Fire Angel
Story of Roxie

From Puppyhood to Adult and Beyond

Nancy Stafford

Copyright © 2019

All Rights Reserved

ISBN: 978-0-9994657-7-6

Dedication

To Laura and Carey who took care of Roxie for many years.

Acknowledgment

To my dad, who gave me Roxie when she was only 6 weeks old. Also, my sister, who was the one who encouraged me to write this book.

About The Author

Nancy Stafford has lived in California all her life, so can be called a true Californian. She has been keeping pets from a young age, from dogs to cats, and even horses. She currently works for Guide Dogs for the Blind National Headquarters, located in San Rafael, California. It has been over 34 years, helping dogs and puppies with their training so that later on, these animals can become guide dogs for the blind and visually impaired.

Nancy loves all her dogs and Roxie was no exception. Her new dog (six months after Roxie) was adopted in June of 2018. Tabi will never replace Roxie. However, Nancy sometimes feels Roxie tells the dog to do things for her. In her free time, Nancy loves to do photography – taking photographs of animals like dogs, horses, and sometimes wild ones. Some of the pictures seen in this book are photographs taken by her.

Contents

Dedication i
Acknowledgment ii
About The Author iii

Chapter 1- Puppy Love 1
Chapter 2- A New Life For Roxie 12
Chapter 3- Mount Tallac 26
Chapter 4- Roxie The Wonder Dog 40
Chapter 5- Loyalty 54
Chapter 6- Strangers 67
Chapter 7- Garbage Dog 80
Chapter 8- Friend 92
Chapter 9- That Crazy Mutt 104
Chapter 10- The Last Days 114

Page Left Blank Intentionally

Chapter 1
Puppy Love

For as long as I could remember, my parents and I always had dogs. I, even as a child, was in love with them. That is the reason I remember most of them very well. I was very young about six years old, when I remember Rags sitting in my father's office. I remember Barney, who was my brother's dog. He had won Barney in a baseball bet.

After that, there was Nicky who was a Labrador retriever that came from Guide Dog; a program for the blind in which Nicky was a participant in 1988. In 1989, he came with my father, which was a career change for Nicky as he was dropped from the program. He died in 2002 and was the last dog we had, before Roxie came into my life.

Around six months after Nicky, in the month of June, I found Roxie. This is the story of *Roxie, the dog*. The dog who came into my life and taught me how to live with patience, while remaining calm and collected. It is the story of Roxie from puppyhood to adult and beyond. With all that she taught me, the joy that she brought, I will never forget this girl as long as I live.

It came to me that every time

I lose a dog; they take

A piece of my heart with them,

And every new dog who comes into

My life gifts me with a piece of their heart

If I live long enough all the components

Of my heart will be dog, and I will become

As generous and loving as they are.

As soon as I took her–the five-week-old puppy–for a walk, I ended up calling her Roxanne; which later changed to Roxie as my neighbors asked me about it, and I realized it had to be a name that my father would remember. The story behind the name is simple and spontaneous. She was named after Roxanne in Cyrano de Bergerac. I named her the first time my dad left her with me, when he went on a vacation. Although I did name her Roxanne, my dad couldn't for the life of him ever remember her full name, so the five-week-old puppy came to be known as Roxie.

Roxie was a dog with a wide range of conflict in her personality. She was protective, yet playful; didn't like strangers, but would dance for some she took a liking to. She was energetic, yet at the same time, she was a couch potato. Most of all, she was loving, generous, and very intelligent. Although I had known a lot of dogs in my life, Roxie was very different from any dog I had yet met. She was by no means a normal, everyday dog.

Roxie was the type of dog that was different in personality from most of the dogs that I have known throughout my life. Sometimes, I would wonder at the vast range of antics that she had learned in such a short amount of time. It seemed to me that Roxie as a mixed breed possessed the energy levels of both the breeds combined. She would always be ready for a walk and most time when we went for a walk, she would be straining on the leash urging me to jog faster and faster until I was sprinting after the mutt. She was very special, a dog who had come to mean the world to me. Dogs are man's best friends. Everyone has heard that, and for me, it is even more of a truth. As a child, it was a revelation to me that dogs could be so loyal and protective. These qualities could be seen very clearly in Roxie. It seemed that when she came to me, she had found the perfect place.

As a mixed breed of Vizsla and Whippet, she was conflicted even in appearance. She was brownish-red in color as Vizsla are prone to be with white markings on her paws and chest, but she was also long-legged like whippets. Roxie had a very short coat of fur and no undercoat at all, so during the cold seasons, I had to buy her a dog jacket or cover her up during the night. She loved to run. When in the mood, she would tear through the condo but most of all she liked to run around trees in big circles, with me chasing behind her.

When I wouldn't chase behind her, she would stand in front of me tail wagging and bark, until I agreed to play her game of chase. Her attitude was also as mixed as her appearance. She was protective and loved to guard her property just like a Vizsla, which is a Hungarian breed of dogs, bred for hunting. Whippets are an English dog breed, also known as the poor man's racehorse because of their running prowess.

Due to this, they are also trained to run after and catch rabbits. Roxie loved to go to the park and she would have the time of her life chasing squirrels. She would literally spend hours chasing them, without showing even the slightest signs of tiring. I would have to drag her away from the park and her squirrels. The squirrels had come to an understanding with Roxie.

Every time we would come to the park, the squirrels would come out and start flitting down from one tree and up the other in a flash, daring Roxie to catch them. I think they all enjoyed their games. Even though she was part Whippet and part Vizsla, who are both supposed to be quiet dogs, Roxie would bark the place down if a stranger would even approach the porch.

It was thanks to her, I would always have a few seconds of forewarning before someone rang the doorbell. Even though Roxie had the qualities of both of the two breeds, she had some traits that were uniquely her own. She loved a tennis ball I got for her. Even when she was fully grown, she would take the ball in her mouth when going out for a walk, and keep it in her mouth the entire time.

If the ball would slip from her teeth, she would just stop and wait for me to put it back in her mouth. She had another habit which was quite prominent, she hated being alone. She wouldn't answer to me if I so much as left her alone for a few minutes in the car, with the windows cracked of course. However, that didn't matter to Roxie, she just wanted to be with someone all the time.

She was also scared of loud noises, especially thunderstorms, she would jump into my lap or curl up next to me on the bed, whenever there was a thunderstorm going on. Along with her loyalty, she was the most playful dog. If she had nothing to do, she would entertain herself by jumping up and down. Each time she would jump, she would try to outdo herself. She was extremely competitive that way.

At the park, she would sprint to her extreme limit if she thought another dog was even thinking about messing with her. I so miss the unique things she used to do that made me fall so much in love with her. I remember the first time I met her, she was five weeks old and living with my dad at his house in Ross, California. She had a sister as well, who was unlike Roxie in color. She was black with a few white markings. Otherwise, they were similar in appearance.

Both of them were five inches in height, long-legged, and slim-built with tiny little feet and ears, and very short fur coats. They were both full of energy that was somehow contagious. When you were in the same room as the both of them, you could not help but want to run and jump just like them. Both of them would get excited at every new thing they saw and would jump around, yapping to each other in puppy language.

They both fed off of each other's energy. If one got excited at something, the other would follow. It was my nephew Billy and his friends, who had found a litter of puppies that someone had just dropped off in the field in a box. They brought the box home, but my brother and his wife told Billy to get rid of them. Billy did not want to leave them outside without anyone to look over them. So, he took the box to my dad's, his grandfather's house. My dad being my dad, was very much in love with having dogs. So he took them in and fixed up a bathroom for them downstairs. If it were not for my nephew, I wouldn't have met Roxie. Soon, I would head over to my father's house in the evenings, to help him with the puppies. It was a lot of work for my dad, taking care of young and energetic puppies all by himself. Billy would come around as well, though he did not know much about puppies.

He would often ask me what they usually ate, what was best for them to eat, what they liked to play with, and so on. I would usually end up reminding him not to add any water to their food, as they did not like it at all. If anyone added water to their food, they would refuse to eat it, then turn up their little noses, and would not even bother looking at it. Roxie and her sister were picky eaters!

It so happened that my dad had planned a trip with his grandchildren to Hawaii, so both Roxie and his sister came to stay with me. I was excited and fixed up my spare bathroom, so they could use it and not spoil the rest of my condominium. I laid down some newspapers and an old bath mat that my father gave me as well.

Let me tell you that those puppies were a handful. Their first visit to the bathroom showed me that I had a lot of work on my hands, in training them to use the facilities properly. All the newspaper I had laid down had been torn up and tossed about the place, the rug had been soiled with poop. Therefore, it was a complete mess. I decided that they needed a crate and I went to Walmart to get one, so that at least they had a proper sleeping area; which to my complete surprise, both of them kept relatively clean.

I remember when I first cut Roxie's nails for her, it was during the time my dad had left her and her sister with me. She was such an excited little puppy that it was a chore getting her to be still enough, so that I could trim the nails without hurting her. All the while, she was trying to get away from my friend and me, who I had called on for help in holding her still. It was one big ordeal that took us most of the afternoon to complete.

We were the whole time either being interrupted by Roxie's sister or by Roxie herself, trying to wriggle free. My dad before leaving had asked me to find a home for Roxie's sister, which I did at a foster care home. Upon his return, Roxie went back to living with my dad. He had also brought a pen for her, so she could play outside. He used to put her in the pen when it came close to the time for me to walk her. One day, as per my routine I came to my dad's house. I saw she was not in her usual place. After looking around the whole property, inside the house, the backyard, and the basement, I got into my car and started driving around the neighborhood. I was calling for her from inside the vehicle at the top of my voice, worried that something might have happened to her.

After all, she was just a puppy and for all her intelligence, she did not know how to look after herself. I was imagining her in the streets somewhere, starting to get hungry, as it was getting close to her feeding time. After searching for a solid hour, I came back dejected. On the way back the only thought I had in my mind was that, maybe she had come back to the condo. As I came to the door expecting to hear her cute little barks, I was sorely disappointed.

My father who was worried as well, came out to check on me, as just one look at my face told him that I was on the verge of tears. I sat down on the porch steps, intending to wait for her a while longer and then going out to the shelters in the neighborhood with her picture, asking if anyone had brought her in, or if anyone had seen her. After half an hour of restless waiting, I heard her tiny little barks. There she was coming up the steps to the back deck from the old horse corral, pelting at full speed towards me. With my heart soaring in the clouds, I ran to grab her before she hurt herself running around helter-skelter. I was surprised by her perseverance. Though she was only eight weeks old, she had not only had managed to escape the pen, she had gone on an adventure, and she had managed to find her way back to her house.

Roxie was one smart puppy! After that day, both my father and I learned our lesson, that Roxie was fond of jumping and adventure. We made it a point to make sure that she was not left in a place, where it was possible for her to jump over anything. We fixed a roof over the pen so that she couldn't jump over it again.

Although this was not the end of our fixing sprees. Roxie's fondness for jumping increased and soon, she had mastered jumping over the fence into the neighbor's garden and running around their property at top speed. After which we had to raise the fence height so that no matter how much older and bigger she got, she was not able to jump over it. It irked her so much that every time she would go into the garden, she would bark at the fence.

Chapter 2
A New Life For Roxie

Roxie lived with my dad for some time, and I used to visit her daily. I was attached to her, even when she did not live with me. So, when my dad decided to sell his house in Ross Calif, he gave Roxie to me. It seemed like a natural decision, seeing that I was already so attached to her and she was to me. She was a shy puppy when it came to people. She would not come up to just anyone. There were only a few selected people who were allowed by Roxie to rub her belly.

When my dad gave Roxie to me, she was still a tiny little puppy. As soon as she came into my home, I had just become her mother and she, my little girl. She had me wrapped around her tiny little paws. Our neighbors who saw Roxie as a puppy wanted her, not only because she was so cute, but also incredibly energetic and lively. Of course, my dad and I didn't want to give her away to anyone. Often when a stranger tried to pet her when she was inside the pen, she always refused to let them even touch her.

That gave me the idea that she would be a good guard dog. Since she was an adorable little puppy, it goes without saying that she was spoiled to the brim. It took me a long time to housebreak her. I brought a crate for her until she was housebroken. Even though I was always patient with her, Roxie was always very sensitive. If you got mad at her for urinating, she would get even worse.

It would then take me hours of playing with her, before she would forget that I had gotten mad. As I said, it was very difficult for me to house-train Roxie. I used to teach her to urinate with the leash on, but she would always forget. This was one thing that I was rather particular about, even when we were indoors. I used to call it her dragging leash. I even asked a friend of mine, who used to take care of her when I was away at work to keep it on her, to take her out this way. The most peculiar thing about Roxie was that she would not do her business, when someone was looking directly at her. So I had to teach my friend not to make direct eye contact with her when they went out for walks. Even I had to be mindful of this. I couldn't look at her directly; otherwise, she would not do anything outside, and soil the condo. She was smart that way. She knew how to train me as well.

However, after I trained her this way, she never urinated in the condominium again, until she was old. She was a kind and funny dog. She loved her jokes and had a lot of fun playing and jumping as high as she could. She taught me to be calm and patient. Whippets are the kinds of dogs that require attention and do not want to be left alone. I used to bring all kinds of stuff for her, and she used to get really excited about it too.

When she found out that I had brought something for her, she would go mad, jumping around the condo and sniffing it, and rolling all over it. She did this the first time I brought something home for her. It was her own pad. She was so excited that she raced around the whole condo, jumping as high as she could go. I loved watching her get this excited about anything I bought for her. She would do the same thing when I brought dog food for her, or chew toys. No matter what it was, she was so used to me bringing things for her that more often than not, she would get excited when I came home with groceries, thinking that I had bought home something new for her. Roxie loved cuddling with me. When she was younger, after I had brought her the pad to sleep on, she used to find any excuse she could, to jump into bed with me. Soon, that became her norm. As she got older, Roxie started using my bed as her own whenever possible.

In the evening after I got home from work, she loved to sit with me on the couch, with her favorite tennis ball clamped in her mouth. Roxie just cuddled with me and wiggled in front of me, trying to get me to rub her belly. When I used to take her on night walks after dinner, she would always take the tennis ball with her, and it used to stay firmly clasped in her mouth the whole time.

She has even developed this funny habit that when the ball would fall out of her mouth, she would just stand and stare at it wagging her tail the whole time. When this happened the first time, thinking that it was her new game, I did not pick up the ball and give it to her. But after a while of staring at the ball and me watching her while she did nothing, she turned to look at me and gave me a tiny little bark. I moved forward, picked up the ball, and offered it to her. She happily took the ball in her mouth and started walking again, pleased with herself. After that she did this every time we used to go out, I was the one who was designated by her to be the one who would always pick up the ball. Whenever I used to take her for her walks, she would be so excited: it was almost her natural state. There were not many things that did not excite her.

Anyways, when I used to take her for the walks at Guide Dogs Ground, she used to put strain on the leash, trying to go ahead and run around. Every time she did this I would have to start running, because I feared that if she strained against the leash anymore, she would hurt herself. After a while, I decided to buy a flexible leash for her. It was made of a very durable elastic material and would stretch for over seven feet.

It gave me a little more room to breathe, and it also allowed Roxie to be as excited as she wanted to be. However, I only got to use the leash for a short time as

Roxie, who did the dandiest things, decided that she liked to chew on her leash. And while doing so, she eventually broke her leash. Even though she was very excited all the time and would sometimes behave like every other dog, she was no ordinary dog. She was my challenge. She would test me to my limits and keep me on my toes in every way possible. She was four months old, when I first took her to work for the first time. To prepare her for the day that she would spend with me at my office, I took her the day before to Guide Dogs for the same time and decided to give her a bath. From my previous experience, I already knew that she did not like baths and as was usual for her, would get excited at it.

So that same thing happened at Guide Dogs, after I was done soaking her, the next thing I know is that she jumped out of the tub just as I was starting to soap her up. She kept doing it the whole time: jumping out of the tub as soon as she got a chance. It took me quite a few tries before she was soap free again. After that day, jumping out of the tub during her bath became her new, favorite thing.

It was almost her habit, that as soon as she was done with her bath, she would wait just long enough for me to put on her collar, and then she would race out to the door and would bark at me, till I came to her with her leash and took her out for a walk. When we were out she would drag me with her and man, was she strong for her size! She used to pull me around and do a takeoff towards the park, where she would spend a happy hour sniffing at tree roots.

Form the time I had known her, she never liked her baths. She would always get impatient, and would wiggle and squiggle around, until I was done. She was always in a hurry to get the bath done. She would almost behave as if she was late for her appointment, which I guess she was. She did have a standing appointment with the park, and all the interesting smells it had to offer. I had a half door in the corridor of my condominium, which I had to fix, as soon as Roxie turned four months old.

Even though the gate was five feet in height and Roxie was about a foot, she could jump over the gate. Before I replaced it, this was her new play. She would jump over it, again and again, getting excited each time that she was able to do it. I could almost feel her astonishment. It seemed to me that even she could not believe that being as tiny as she was, she could jump that high.

However, to prevent Roxie from injuring herself, I

added a gate on top of it, so that it was at least eight feet in height. After only a span of a few months, she was up over that gate too. When I had added a gate on top of the one she could jump, Roxie was mad at me for days. She would not play with me. And if I insisted that she plays with me, she would just go and stand in front of the door, and bark at it.

Despite her anger, she couldn't keep from the challenge for very long. She was soon trying to jump higher than she previously could. As she was still growing, it was not hard for her to improve her jumps, as she got bigger and bigger. Hence, after a few months to her utter surprise and my exasperation, she had succeeded in jumping over the new gate as well. After this incident, I had to stop using a gate altogether. This crazy dog of mine really knew how to jump. She was not the one to shy away from a challenge.

When I started training her, I found that she was really smart. After only a few days, she was responding to simple commands like sit, lie down, and roll over. So when she was around seven months old, I started teaching her more tricks. And boy was she a fast learner! She completely swept me off my feet with her agility and cleverness.

I taught her the best tricks, like jumping hoops and

putting up different paws when asked. She learned to recognize which paw to lift up when I said *"left"* or *"right"*, as she would pick up the correct paw in response. I even taught her to lift her right paw, when she met someone, in greeting. Another trick that I taught her was jumping on my back when I was on my knees. When she was seven months old, she was light enough that I could have her jump on my back, landing squarely on my back, with the impact of her full weight. The first time I taught her hoop jumping, I put the hoop in the doorway of my bedroom, and used her favorite treat to get her to walk through the hoop. When she would comply, I would give her the treat. After a few months of this, I raised the height of the hoop to a foot above the ground and had her jump through it for some time.

When she had perfected jumping through the hoop at the height of one foot, I raised the hoop three feet high and had her jump through that, giving her a treat each time which excited her to no end. I was doing her favorite thing with her and was giving her favorite treat to her for doing something she would have done for free. She was in doggy heaven. Since she loved jumping, she perfected the jumps I was teaching her, and also learned to jump through two hoops at once, both vertical.

Next, I taught her the trick of jumping on my back and laying there for a while before jumping down. I would get down on my knees and place a treat in my hand that I had raised above my head. Roxie had no choice but to jump on my back to reach my hand. If she did what I wanted her to do, she would get two treats; one that she would eat from my hand after jumping on my back, and the other if she waited before jumping back down. Since she was a smart dog, who wanted to eat a lot of treats, she got the hang of the game very soon. The one thing that Roxie was scared off, was strangers coming to the condo. This made her an excellent guard dog. She did not like it when strangers would come up to her and pet her. She was, however, not shy about airing her opinions, and would bark furiously at anyone, who would try to come up to her to pet her.

She was very protective of her property and me. She knew what was hers and she would not let anyone else touch it. Although I did like that she would give me warnings if someone was approaching the condo, I also wanted her to be friendly, at least a little bit, when my friends came over. So to get her somewhat used to people, I decided to take her to work one day, and had everyone come up to her and pet her.

She did not like that one bit. She spent the whole day turning her behind, on people who came up to her, and she made everyone scratch her bum for her. Everyone was amused by her antics. Whenever someone came up to her and scratch her behind, she would do a funny little dance for them, but she never let anyone pet her. The crazy mutt had a sense of humor as well.

There was this one incident, when she was only a few months old. I had her in a crate, and I needed to do some shopping. It was too warm for me to leave her in the car, so I took her to an antique store opposite the shop, and she stayed there in her crate. She was about four months old, and for the duration of my shopping, the store owner was watching her for me. Ever since that first time, she loved going to that store and staying with the owner, when I went to get my shopping done.

Another time, I left her in the car in a shaded area for just a little while. Roxie was protecting my car when a couple of teenage boys happened to pass near it. Even though they were just passing, Roxie, possibly as a defense mechanism started barking as though she would bite them the first chance she got. She did not like it one bit, if I left her alone. Considering the fact that I had previously asked the boys not to approach the car when I was away, they also got their lesson.

When she was around five months old, I hired a dog sitter and a dog walker for her, so I did not have to take her to work every day, especially when I had to work at night. Laura, the dog sitter, at that time lived next door to me, so it was easy for me to take Roxie over to her condo. She was very good with Roxie, and they both got along very well. In fact, I felt that Roxie liked Laura more than me sometimes. Roxie showed her preference for Laura in different ways. Sometimes, when all three of us would go out for a walk and I would pull a little ahead of Laura, Roxie would pull me up short, so that she could catch up.

When Roxie was around six months old, Laura took a picture of her, running around in the grass very fast. That crazy mutt would chase her as she ran the circles full blast. She would sometimes stop and wait for us to come and get her; and then she would start running in circles again, as fast as she could go. If there were trees in the area, she would run around them, weaving in and out among the trees in figure eight.

Another picture that I love was taken by a friend of mine, who passed away two years ago, when Roxie was about 10 months old. It was the first time my friend met her, and the crazy mutt only let her pet her behind as usual. Once I got her back into the car, my friend went up to the car to get a picture of her sitting on the driver's side. Roxie did not like that one bit. She barked at my friend to let her know that she was too close to the car.

Among the things Roxie loved to do, one was to sit on the driver side of the car whenever I had to go into the store. So one day in a spontaneous bout of creativity, I took a picture of her and made it into a poster reading *"Foxie Roxie Taxi Cab, you want a ride I drive 12 milk bones a mile"*. I loved taking pictures of her, and she loved to pose for me just as much. I remember one time when I took her to work with me, and I had her on a tie-down.

There were some sweet cookies on the desk, and all she had to do was put her paw on the desk to take them. She almost finished half the plate before I had pushed the dish back, so she could not reach them anymore. I also recall that there was another time at my dad's place in Greenbrae, when we were having dinner and young Roxie, who was about 8 months old snuck into the kitchen, to investigate what was in the garbage bag.

I brought her out of there and put her on my lap, as soon as I was distracted when the dinner was served, Roxie took the first opportunity to sneak back into the kitchen. And the next time I went to look for her, she was having a feast on my dad's kitchen floor. I had to mop the whole floor. This time Roxie knew she was in trouble, so before I even had the chance to scold her, she ran back out into the dining room.

She sat down under the dining table, right by my seat with her head between her paw and a sad expression on her face; indicating to me with the big puppy eyes that she didn't want to get scolded, right after she had the time of her life. Of course, I didn't scold her. But after this incident at my dad's place, I always kept the garbage bag on the top counter at my home. Even then, she would come into the kitchen every now and then, and look for stuff in it, as an adult.

Roxie did have some problems as a puppy, but she outgrew most but not all of them. Years ago, I had an artist do a picture of Roxie which shows off her soft face and warm brown eyes. Every time I used to see those eyes, I would get a warm fuzzy feeling inside. I still do, every time I recall her face, the feeling returns. I miss her warm eyes and her pink nose. She was so special to me.

Chapter 3
Mount Tallac

When Roxie was seven months old, I started teaching her all sorts of tricks. Since she was a very smart dog, she was quick to grasp. By the time she was one, she had learned enough and was able to show off these tricks in front of people. One of her favorite tricks was to jump on my back, when I bent over and I placed a cookie there for her. As time went on and she repeated the trick, she got so good with it that she would jump on my back, as soon as I bend over. One dog year is equal to seven human years, and even though Roxie was still young by human standards, she had grown into a beautiful long-legged dog. She was active as a puppy, and she was no different as an adult. In fact, she seemed to have become more active and energetic.

She ran even faster, and jumped higher than ever. She could easily scale 10 feet high fences, which was no problem for her. However, as a one year old, Roxie did not like company. She was a possessive dog, who did not trust easily. So to make her feel more at ease among people, I decided to take her to different places. One place that we both used to love going to, was the retirement home.

It was there Roxie learned that not all people were terrible, and that she could trust people. Slowly, she started loosening up and would let people pet her back sometimes. In one of the rest homes that we went, there was an activities director named Jamie, who gave Roxie the nickname, Roxie the wonder dog. This name stuck with her for the rest of her life. She was indeed a wonder dog. To me, she still is a wonder dog.

She forged such a deep connection with me that to this day, I remember her with fondness, and it is still difficult for me to have lost her. She was docile and friendly with me in every sense of the word. It seemed to me that she was meant to be with me, that is how perfectly we lived together. After the first few trips to the retirement home, Roxie started looking forward to going there. She used to get really excited every time we went.

Soon, she was entertaining the residents of the retirement home with all the tricks that she had learned from me. The residents loved to see a dog performing for them as well. So, it became our custom to visit the retirement home, at least once a month. Later on, we included other rest homes in our circuit, ones throughout Marin and Sonoma Counties as well. Roxie was a dog who loved to get attention. She just gobbled up praise.

After she performed a trick well, she would look around, as if she was expecting applause, which I must say she usually got from the onlookers. This used to amuse her a lot, and she would then run around the room jumping and showing off even more, and people would laugh even harder at her antics. So it followed, my life was affected by Roxie so much that it seemed to me that she was meant to be a part of my life. There were so many things that she did that just naturally became a part of my life. For example, she would usually jump into bed with me, even though she had her own bed. That transition was so seamless, as both of us just felt a natural affinity towards each other. It was even more enhanced by the fact that Roxie was a selective dog. She would not let just anybody pet her or get close to her, even as a young puppy.

However, she was open and playful with me. Although, that did change sometimes, especially when I left her alone. It so happened that around the time Roxie turned one, my sister invited me to her house for Thanksgiving. We both talked over the phone about it and discussed everything. During the conversation, my sister mentioned that it would be better if I didn't bring Roxie over, as she had just gotten a new dog who was very aggressive.

Since Roxie was also very possessive, she did not want a dogfight to happen, neither did she want either of the dogs to get hurt because of the other. I agreed with her sentiments. I was very fond of Roxie and did not want anything bad happening to her. Since I loved dogs in general, I did not want anything to happen to Rocco, my sister's dog, as well. Thinking that the party was only going to be a couple of hours, I left Roxie at the condo. When I reached my sister's house, however, the party was in full swing, and what was supposed to be two hours turned into eight. On the way home, I remember that I was anxious to get back to home knowing that Roxie had been alone in the condo, and I had never left her alone for this long. So I hurried. As soon as I got home and opened the door, I knew I was right to feel anxious. It was as if we were connected.

I was able to feel Roxie's anxiety. She came flying out the condo, as soon as she heard me turn the key in the lock. That dog sometimes did things that made me feel like I was living with a child instead of a pet, and I loved her like a child too. I had picked her up, and then I entered the house and closed the door. Roxie had almost scratched the paint off the front door. There were claw marks all over the door as if she had wanted to get out.

I think if I had been a few hours late she would have actually managed to find a way out. This was when I discovered that Roxie had separation anxiety. She did not like being left alone. If I left her alone for a little while, she would try to act as if she was mad at me; but this time when

I got back from the party, she did not do that. I think she was very glad to see me. I also think she had thought that I had abandoned her or something. That thought wrenched my heart and after that, I made sure not to ever leave her alone for that long. Roxie was almost one and a half when she took her first trip with me. I took her to the mountains, north of Lake Donner. That morning, I was excited about my first trip with my baby. She was very sensitive to my emotions by then, and caught on my excitement. When I was preparing breakfast for us that morning, she stood in the kitchen and looked at me as though saying, *"What surprises have you got up your sleeve this morning, huh mommy?"*

Her looks sometimes spoke volumes, and I felt compelled to answer her, so I said to her with a giggle, *"You just wait and see Roxie, I have a right surprise for you, today we are going to do all the walking you can dream off."* After which I laid down her breakfast in her bowl and sat down to have mine, all the while talking excitedly with her. After I had finished eating my breakfast, I looked down at Roxie's bowl which was almost full. I had gotten her too excited, and now all she wanted to do was run and jump.

Shaking my head exasperatedly as well as lovingly at my mutt, I picked up her bowl and went to the kitchen to pack up the breakfast for her, so she could have it after the hike. We started the hike and made it to the top of a big hill, from which we had a magnificent view of the surroundings. By that time Roxie was really hungry. She was constantly coming up to me and sniffing the bag in which I had packed her breakfast, and giving me a look that said, *"Okay you were right, this is a lot of walking, now I am hungry. Feed me."*

That look she gave me, made me laugh. I told her that as soon as we got to the top, we would stop for a rest, and then she could have her breakfast. As soon as I sat down Roxie came and plopped down in front of me, her tongue hanging out in anticipation of her meal. As soon as I had put it in front of her, she gobbled it all up in no time. This trip to the mountains was the first time Roxie had seen snow. Her reaction when she came into contact with the cold white powder was hilarious.

She gave me comical looks while playing with enthusiasm in the snow, having the time of her life. Even though she did not like water, she was entranced by the snow. She was soon jumping up and down, to catch the snowflakes in her mouth. I took her to Soda Springs Lake, and just above Soda Springs, I let her loose with the snow, and she ran through it with snow flying everywhere, having the best time of her life. After a while of playing with her, we got back in the car and headed to my brother's place, located in Truckee, California, a few miles from Soda Springs. When I got there, Roxie and I unloaded the car and went inside.

As soon as we were inside, Roxie started shaking the water off of her coat, and I hurried to take out her towel so that I could dry her off. This weather was colder than what she was habitual of, and I did not want her getting sick on the trip. I wanted both of us to enjoy our time together. My brother got us something to eat, a coffee with sandwiches for me and doggy biscuits for Roxie, which again she ate very quickly. She was hungry after a full morning of running around in the snow. I was glad to see that she had a good appetite. I had been worried that traveling would not agree with her, since she was a sensitive dog.

However, she seemed to be enjoying immensely. Although, there was a little hitch. As soon as we entered my brother's house, Roxie had been bothered by the noise of the heater. She did not like the loud noise, and the blowing sound of the heater was setting her on edge. So to get her settled down, I had my brother turn the heater off for a while. As soon as the heater was off, she jumped off my lap and went to investigate the heater, sniffing all around it. This was her go-to response to any and all loud noises, to jump on my lap.

As bedtime got closer and I prepared myself for bed, Roxie took it upon herself to climb on my bed and snuggle under the covers, waiting for me to lie down with her. She was always looking for the opportunity to climb into bed with me. She did not like sleeping alone, especially as the heater was on again for the night and she was still not fully comfortable with it. I also did not want her off my bed, as it was a cold night and the added warmth of Roxie's furry little body was comforting. So we both went to sleep, tired after our day's adventures.

After a few days, we packed up our stuff, I said goodbye to my brother, and Roxie and I headed for South Lake Tahoe and the Fallen Leaf Lake. I asked my brother for directions, and he told me there were two ways to get to there. One was a shorter route, but the other, longer route was more picturesque. So naturally, I took the longer route, thoroughly enjoying myself with Roxie. She was having a good time too, with her head hanging outside the window, looking in fascination at the countryside flashing past her. It took us five hours to get there from Truckee, but we were not in any hurry, so we did not feel as if it was a very long time, especially since the views were amazing.

I was to meet my sister at South Lake Tahoe, but she was late in getting there. So instead of waiting for her, I decided to unpack in the cabin and make it look nice, so that all of us could have a nice time with each other. Since I was unpacking, and was afraid Roxie would get into someplace and hurt herself, I left her in the car. During my unpacking, my sister also arrived and we both unpacked together. As soon as we were done with unpacking, we gave the cabin a careful look-over, to make sure there was nowhere that Roxie could get to and end up hurting herself. After we were sure that no such thing was going to happen, we let her out.

As soon as she was out of the car, Roxie, in true Roxie fashion darted past both of us and into the cabin, and started sniffing at all the new smells. After she was done sniffing and investigating the cabin, she sat down on the couch and settled down to take a nap. I think that was Roxie's way of telling us that she liked the place, or maybe she was just tired. So, assuming that she should have a proper place to sleep in the cabin, I unpacked her bed for her and laid it down in my bedroom. Even though she loved her bed, when it came time to go to bed, like I said Roxie would always try to get into bed with me. The bed I had at the cabin was very small.

However, that was not enough of a reason to make her change her mind. After two days at the cabin, my sister took Roxie and me for hiking to the top of Mount Tallac. As soon as we made it to the upper Cathedral Lake, Roxie started coming up to me, sniffing at my bag again, with a look clear on her face that said, *"Feed me."* As soon as we got to the Lake, I gave her packed breakfast, and she hadn't had any that morning, she was starving, and in a style that was much unlike her, she ate her breakfast in no time at all. She usually took her time with eating. She would never eat in one go. She was also a very picky eater and hated soggy meals.

She preferred her meals to be dry, and even though I gave her proper meals, the rascal always wanted to go dumpster diving. I even caught her going through my kitchen garbage. After all of us were done with our post hiking snacks, we got up to head back down the trail. My sister Mary and Roxie went ahead, almost running down the trail, while I followed the two of them down at a much slower pace. When I got to the bottom, I found them sitting on the rocks, at the end of the trail.

When I approached them, Roxie looked up at me with a look on her face that clearly said, *"Mom, what took you so long, we have been waiting for so long!"* All her looks were comical because they were so spot on. I told her that I was enjoying the view, at which Roxie just looked at me like okay, but the smells here are more interesting. As soon as she gave me that look, I burst into giggles.

My sister and everyone close to me respected the relationship that I had with Roxie. They knew that the two of us shared a special bond, and no one made fun of me, when I talked like this to Roxie. They could all see as well that the expression that Roxie gave me, were clearly communicative. They all knew her to be a smart dog with whom you could almost carry out a conversation.

After going down the trail, I was feeling a bit hot, so I decide to go to the docks and let my feet dangle in the waters of the Fallen Leaf Lake, which was very near our cabin. The first thing Roxie does after I had settled down with my feet dangling in the water, is to take a flying leap straight into the cold water of the lake. Now, Roxie is by no means a water dog. She doesn't even like taking baths. I do not know what she was thinking, when she took the flying leap and jumped in one of the coldest lakes in the region. As soon as the water hit her, she came swimming back to me in a hurry, to get out of the lake. After this incident, she learned her lesson for life, and never again took flying leaps into any body of water.

We had a great time hiking in the mountains together. So I made a thing out of it and again took Roxie to the mountains. The next time both of us went to the cabin at

South Lake Tahoe, we explored another trail of Mount Tallac. At the top of this trail, we discovered a waterfall and a creek. I thought it would be a great idea to go across the creek and continue up the trail. Roxie, however, refused to cross the creek. I even found a log that she could walk on to go across, but still, she refused. Finally, I settled myself and Roxie on a rock next to the creek, and ate lunch with her. When we got back to the cabin, Roxie was one tired dog.

She ate her dinner and immediately went to bed. The next day, we walked to the store down the road, and I taught Roxie to stay on the side of the road, because it was very narrow. Being a smart dog she quickly picked up on it, and whenever we used to visit the cabin, she would always walk on the side.

I was always glad that Roxie picked up on instructions like these, since they could save her life. I never wanted her to be in any sort of danger, so I was always teaching her stuff that could prevent her from getting into trouble. She was a very cautious dog, always sniffing, and never going too far away from me. I think she thought that she was my protector and that made her stick close to me, and for that, I was very happy.

FIRE ANGEL STORY OF ROXIE

Chapter 4
Roxie The Wonder Dog

After our first trip to the mountains, I made sure to take Roxie up there regularly. She had such a good time on that first trip that I wanted to make this trip with her, again and again. It made me happy that Roxie was having a good time. So, I took her there for the next seven years.

After I taught her to walk on the side of the road while heading to the store, she never did stray from that practice again. I remember on one trip, when both of us had walked down to the store, and I took some pictures of her while she was laying down on the docks. I was looking out with my camera in hand, trying to take a picture of the lake; when I happened to turn around and there was Roxie, sitting on the docks perfectly outlined by the sun.

She just looked so amazing that I automatically snapped the first picture of her, thinking that she would move soon. When she did not move, seeing that I was taking pictures of her (she always did love to pose). I focused more clearly and snapped a few more shots of her. They came out beautiful. The amber color of the sun was illuminating Roxie's red-brown coat, and made her look like a beautiful diva ready to catwalk.

I remember the last hike I took Roxie on. It was to the lower part of Cathedral Lake. She, as usual, had a lot of fun hiking. Coming down from the lake, I fell on some loose rocks that were scattered on the trail and hurt my knee. Roxie, the ever protective companion, made sure that I was okay and she even slowed down her pace to walk beside me slowly, so that I might not strain my knee too much by walking quickly. After we got to the car, I realized that I was too sore to go and make dinner for us, so I decided to drive to town and get some pizza. However, I made sure that I gave Roxie her dinner. Like I have said, Roxie was a picky eater. She did not like everything and mostly ate only a little at a time. She would leave her meal halfway through and then I would pack up the rest, which she would eat a little later. She always finished her meals, but she usually ate them in installments.

After I got back from town with the pizza, I was so sore that I had to crawl up the steps to the cabin. That night, Roxie slept with me on the bed. Although she was such a caring dog that she avoided getting near my bad knee, the whole night. The next morning, I got up, packed our stuff, and made sure I packed Roxie's belongings as well. After completing these tasks, I took Roxie for a short walk since I was still sore from yesterday's fall.

After the walk, we took our luggage out to the car and said goodbye to the cabin. That was the last time I was up there with Roxie, and I still miss going to the cabin with her. I have not been back at the cabin after she passed away. Although, I think someday I will go there again without her. There is a church out there, where I think I will plant a marker at the resting site and inscribe it with Roxie's name, so that her name could always be up there. I still miss her so much and sometimes, the memories I have of Roxie are so vivid that I feel as if she will come running up the driveway. Sometimes, I feel that she will jump up on the couch with me and perform a trick for me. I miss her tricks most of all. She had gotten so good with them. I began teaching her tricks when she was just a few months old, but when she was around two, I used to take her to the retirement homes so that she would perform for the elderly; and make them laugh and help them have a good time.

Roxie was all for making people have a good time. However, the only condition for that was, she should like them too. She used to love performing in the retirement homes and even liked going there. There was one retirement home called Tamalpais, located on the Via Casitas in Greenbrae that she was particularly fond of. I think the reason for that was that the activities manager there had given her the nickname Roxie the wonder dog, which she was very fond of, as I have already described earlier.

I even got a tag made for her collar that read *"Roxie the Wonder Dog"*. The collar on which I put the tag on, was also really nice. Roxie liked it as the best out of all her collars. The color of the collar was red and black. However, I think the reason that Roxie was fond of the collar was that it was made out of deer hide and was soft, unlike most collars that were made of leather. That collar is now in my cabinet, while her leash hangs on the door of my bedroom.

I always liked buying new stuff for her. Her excitement over getting new things was palpable, and I could not help myself. When she went out to perform, I thought a shiny collar would look much more appropriate on her. So I had a new collar made out of rhinestones for her. She was jumping with joy at having gotten a shiny, new thing. I was happy by seeing her jump up and down, a dozen times a second.

She performed all over Marin County and parts of Sonoma wearing her new collar that she loved to put on, as much as she loved putting on performances. Roxie performed her tricks for around seven years, and in that time, she even became accomplished at performing tricks that I have never seen any other dog master. For example, Roxie was a pro at jumping through hoops, both vertical and horizontal, and even two at a time.

She was extremely good with the first trick that she ever learned, jumping over my back while I bend over, laying there and then jumping off. She even knew the difference between her right and left paw. However, the trick that she loved performing was taking a bow. When she would bow to the audience after a performance, it would make people laugh and be impressed with her; and she would get a lot of praise from them. They would want to pet her, and take a lot of pictures of her.

They would give her treats, and she liked all the attention diverted towards her, after taking a bow. When she was younger, Roxie was a little less disciplined, and she used to run all over the house getting excited over the little things. As a young puppy, I remember, Roxie used to love running up the stairs in front of my condo at full speed; after reaching the top in a matter of seconds, she would graciously stop for me and when I got up there, we would continue on our long hike to Bon Air Shopping Center.

From there, the two of us would head over to the lagoon, and from there we would call it a day and head back home. It was during one of these walks that we met a lady who owned a Labrador. We saw that she was throwing a tennis ball for her dog and was bragging about how fast her dog was. After hearing her talk, I challenged her and took Roxie's leash off. Then I had her throw the ball and both the dogs bounded after it. Roxie beat her dog to the ball and back without breaking a sweat, and her dog did not even come close to beating my girl. The look on the woman's face was priceless and I was so proud of Roxie for winning the impromptu race. She was a smart dog and knew she had to win. There was very little that escaped her notice. Even though the woman's dog was larger than Roxie, she defeated her Labrador.

When the woman looked at Roxie with an incredulous expression on her face, I mentioned that Roxie was part Whippet. That was one of Roxie's Shining moments among many others. There were so many things Roxie did that were unique only to her. One of the things she loved to do when the two of us would go somewhere in the car was getting into the passenger side of the car and then, laying down on the floor with her head on the shift board. I used to adore it when she looked at me, while I was driving the car.

Roxie was always a cautious dog. So, when we reached someplace and I had to leave her in the car, she would never jump out and wander about, even though I left all the windows open. I did that because I was always worried about the car overheating and making Roxie sick. I was glad that Roxie was sensible to this and would not jump out of the car. What she did, however, was get into the driver's seat as soon as I was out of the car, and sit there waiting for me to return as if she was the driver, and was about to drive me off to my next destination.

I always found that pose of hers funny. I imagined her wearing a chauffeur's hat and sitting in the driver's seat, and it would give me the giggles. One time when I got out of the car I remembered to open all the windows, but forgot to close the driver side door. I went into the store and did my shopping, when I came out I noticed that the car door was open.

I rushed to the car, thinking that surely Roxie would have climbed out by now, but there she was sitting in her usual spot on the passenger side floor, with her head on the car shift looking at me with the expression that plainly said, *"Mom, you forgot to close the car door, you know that right?"* There was only one incident in all the time that I took Roxie out in the car that she ever jumped out of the car. That was so unusual for her that both my sister and I concluded that someone must have tried to get in and it scared her. Even then, she did not wander far. My little girl was the most sensible dog I had ever met. She knew I worried about her and so she would make sure that even while she was chasing squirrels in the park, not to stray far from me.

Since I worked for Guide Dogs and it was my job to take care of them, I would sometimes bring some of my charges over. Roxie would have a great time playing with them. She even boded with some of them and made good friends. One of the dogs that I took care of, was a retired breeder named Natoma. She was a yellow Labrador who loved to follow Roxie around.

Roxie, who was very self-assured, loved this and by extension, formed a good companionship with Natoma over the years. However, Roxie was not one to stand for rude behavior from anyone, not even if they were well liked by her. So, once Natoma was trying to jump up on an old lady, for some unfathomable reason, and Roxie got between her and the lady and barked at Natoma.

She sounded like she was scolding her and saying, *"Don't do that, it is rude!"*

Roxie was a leader and had a way of making people and dogs fall in line. There was no way that Natoma was going to argue with her. She even learned some tricks while she was trying to copy Roxie. Once I remember she was watching Roxie jump through some hoops, and she decided to try it for herself.

After doing it a few times, she seemed to like doing it and after she went back to her keeper, she showed off the new trick she had learned. After that, whenever I took care of Natoma, she came with Roxie and me to a few of the shows that we went to. We took her with us until she passed away at the age of 12. Natoma liked to chase cats, and it was hilarious to watch her while she did so.

Roxie, however, would sit on the side and just watched Natoma's antics. Roxie never chased a cat her entire life.

She would go up to and sniff them, if they let her, otherwise, she just let them be. There was one incident that I remember where a cat was teasing Roxie; after a little while of ignoring from Roxie, the cat teased her a little more and ran under my car.

All Roxie did was put her head under the car, and just gave one bark. That was all it took for the cat to scatter and not repeat the incident. Despite Roxie's disinterest in chasing cats, she was interested in chasing some other small, furry animal; squirrels. They would tease her and run up the trees, and Roxie would try to climb up after them. Although she did get a bit further up than most dogs could, the squirrels were more nimble on the trees and Roxie never managed to catch one.

Even though Roxie was an energetic dog, who liked to take care of others before herself, she did have a few moments where she decided to look after herself first. I was very surprised and pleased whenever she decided to do that. It was so humane of her that I fell even more in love with my companion. Roxie continued to perform at retirement homes for seven years, after which I retired her when she was almost nine years old.

The reason I retired her was that she had hurt herself during a show jumping through one of the hoops, and did not want to perform any of the harder tricks after that. That is why I am saying that she sometimes behaved so much like an actual human that it really surprised me. She used to look at me and sometimes her expressions used to convey her feelings, like she was speaking with words. After the accident, Roxie looked at me with the expression that said, *"I don't want to do this anymore, I just want to spend time with you. This makes me tired."* There was another dog that I used to bring home, that is, before the Guide Dogs implemented a rule that employees could not take any active dogs to their homes. Roxie and Ned got along well, and she enjoyed playing with Ned and Felix. Ned was Felix's Guide Dog. Both of them enjoyed Roxie's company.

She was just so adorable when she had friends to play with, she would go wild, running, and jumping up and down. However, she would also make sure that those who she was with were behaving themselves. She would never let anyone get away with any rude behavior. She was always the most gentle and kindest of all the dogs that I have known. This is another aspect of her that I miss a lot.

Roxie was a free spirit, and I think that is the reason she did not like kennels. And also she did not like being separated from me. She hated to be locked up, that was just something that was not for her at all. She would always be annoyed that she had been put into a kennel, and would be glad whenever she was let out. She would do the usual stuff, go running around in circles and jump as high as she could, to show her joy at being let out. Whenever she was locked inside, she would do anything that she could to try getting out. She even broke her teeth while she tried chewing on the bars. I had to get them replaced several times. She would not care for anything, once she set her mind to something. Hence, when she had set her mind to getting out of the kennel, she did not care about herself, she just tried everything she could to get out. I also tried using a bitter spray to discourage her from trying to chew on the bars and breaking her teeth, but it was all to no avail.

When Roxie wanted something, she would not let something like a bitter spray deter her from her goal. Roxie would lose her well-maintained composure, whenever she was at the kennels. She would bark and chew on the wire when she was outside and once she was let in, she would immediately want to be let out again. I think she thought it was some kind of a game. Opening the door and going in and out, never staying in one place. She was sometimes funny in the way she understood the world.

To make her feel more comfortable in the kennels, I wrote a note to the head of staff there, and asked him to inform all the employees that I would be the one cleaning her stall and no one else should do it. I had the idea that Roxie might not get too upset, if I cleaned her stall with *"accel cleaner"*. The idea worked, Roxie never chewed on the bars again. However, I still was not able to put in any bedding inside the stall, as she would shred it up and scatter it all over the stall.

Even though I loved her a lot, she was sometimes a brat, and I did not mind it at all. I liked that she had such a versatile personality, and so many likes and dislikes. Another one of her dislikes was that she did not like to eat wet food, she liked her food dry and in small portions distributed over the whole day. And she would always be ready for her treats. I loved her little quirks with all my heart, and it is the small things about her that I miss so much.

Chapter 5
Loyalty

Roxie was like a friend to me. I would take her for walks and talk to her the whole day. I would even get jealous sometimes when she showed more attention to someone else. Although Roxie was picky, she did not do it often. She was very much attached to her sitter Laura. The show-off would jump and bark excitedly, whenever Laura would come over. She would also jump up and down in excitement, and sometimes even try to jump on to her. When Roxie was done showing her excitement, she would obediently go over to the door of my condo and wait patiently for Laura to come over, tie the leash onto her collar, and take her for a walk.

Walks with Roxie were always filled with funny incidents. Sometimes, she would run around in the park making us run after her. Her favorite thing to do was run very fast in one direction, and when Laura or I would start chasing her, she would change her direction very fast. This would begin as a game that would only end, if Roxie would let us catch her.

Otherwise, she would just keep running until we were tired, and would just sit down to catch a breath. Every time this happened, Roxie would come to sit beside us, panting herself. Even if she was tired, she would never let a squirrel go by without giving it a little chase. She was always ready for a chase and a walk. I would take her for the longest walks ever. She liked it and got very excited, when I took different routes every night.

This gave her new things to explore. Sometimes, she was the one who decided which route she wanted to take. She would get ahead of me, and navigate the streets all by herself. After the long walks, when she would finally be near the point of getting tired, she would turn around, and start walking the way we had come. It was her way of telling me that she was ready to go home and sleep. I was sure she knew her way back home, and she would be able to get back without much difficulty.

There were so many things that she did that made me think that I was living with a person, and not just a pet. She was the perfect blend of a kind, happy, and quirky dog. I was delighted that she came in my life. She made me turn into a much calmer and patient person. I had become much more productive and had started being much more aware of time, since I had to make sure that I did everything on time for Roxie. I took her for her walks on time and gave her meals punctually.

Meals were a bit of a challenge with Roxie. She was a picky eater and used to have small meals. In addition to having a small meal, Roxie was also prone to throw up, if she missed a meal. If I didn't give her breakfast and took her for a drive, she was likelier to throw up. That was the reason I always kept a packed meal for her, whenever I took her out with me. This was another thing about Roxie, she was always ready to go out with me. I had started looking for more and more places that allowed pets to accompany their owners. There were only a few shops that I went to, that did not allow pets to enter. When this would happen, I would leave Roxie at the neighboring shops, and they were pleased to have her every time.

I observed that when I was not around, Roxie was a well-behaved dog. It was only my presence that made her act out, and turn into a goofy dog that would jump all over the place. She was always more thrilled in my presence, and she would make sure that I knew it. Jumping up and down and wagging her tail a lot are a few examples. But all these things made me feel like I was her world, as much as she had become mine.

She was the one that I was always worried about. I would be shopping, and I would look at stuff and think that Roxie would look good wearing that hat or that scarf. More often than not, I would end up buying it for her. She showed so much enthusiasm whenever I brought over something for her, that it made me want to buy her something new every now and then, so that I could just see her elated. I must say, my excitement of having her around, did not go away as well. It is the excitement that you get when something new enters your life. Well, I got that when Roxie came over to live with me for the first time. But the thing is, it actually never went away. It always remained. All the time that Roxie was with me, I felt like it was an adventure. As I said, she would do the darndest things, and then pretend like she just hadn't done it.

For she knew some of the things she did would upset me a little, and I would become even more conscious about taking care of her. Once, Roxie decided that she wanted to go on an adventure alone. I did not know what thought took hold of her. I was on the computer in my room, and had left Roxie in the living room. She was sitting on the couch the way she liked to do, especially in the afternoon.

Anyways, while I was on the computer, I thought to myself that it was about time for Roxie's walk, and that I should probably take her before she got excited, and started running around the house. So, I put away my keyboard and went to the living room. The first thing I noticed was that the couch was empty and before I could start looking around the condo, I noticed that the entrance screen door was open.

That excitable dog had taken it upon herself to go out, and take her walk alone. I did not know why she would do that. I immediately rushed outside and started looking for her. After about half an hour of searching, I called my dad at his house, although that too was of no help, as she had not come his way as well. By this time, I was worried. Since the incident when she was living with my dad as a puppy, Roxie had never gone alone outside. It was something that had made me very happy and relaxed.

However, now I was worried, as it had occurred for the first time. Where would she go? I decided to look for her at her favorite park as well. I didn't even want to think about the possibility that she might not be there. However, as soon as I got out of my condo, she was standing outside, near the ivy where she liked to pee. I was sure that she had not been there, when I had gotten out of the condo and started looking for her.

The darn dog was playing with my mind, and making me worry about her. I went to her, and looked at her. She was sitting up on her back legs, looking at me with puppy eyes, as she knew she had done something to upset me. It was true I was upset with her, but only because I thought that something might happen to her, if she went out without me.

I did not like to curb her natural curiosity, as I liked it; it made her who she was. So, I tried not to scold her too much when things like this happened. Although, I did make sure after that incident never to leave the screen door open. I did not want Roxie wandering around on the streets. Even though she was a smart dog, accidents could happen to anyone. People these days are very careless, especially young drivers. They would just hit Roxie and run away. I did not like to even think about it. It gave me chills down my spine, and I just made sure that I locked the screen door after that incident.

Her going out alone was certainly not the norm, it was an isolated incident. When I took her in the car, she would stay put, even when I rolled down all the windows and went shopping, I would come back to find Roxie in the driver's seat looking like a chauffeur and looking at me as though asking me, *"Where to next, ma'am?"* I always found it hilarious whenever I came back to the car to find Roxie in the driver's seat with that expression. She would know that I was laughing at her antics, so she would then get up and wag her tail for me, with her tongue hanging out looking as though she was laughing at herself.

Like I have already said, Roxie was the kind of dog that did not get along well with strangers. She would bark at them and would not let them come near her, if she did not like them. She was very protective of me as well. Once, I had gone grocery shopping and had brought a lot of stuff, a clerk came out to the car to help put everything in the car. When he saw Roxie in the driver's seat, she started tapping the back window to get her attention as he wanted to say hello.

Roxie did not like that and was ignoring him. So I told him that I would bring her out of the car if he would go wait by the window, as Roxie was a little sensitive and did not meet strangers right away. When I took Roxie out and walked her over to the clerk, she took one look at him and gave one big loud bark, as if to say, *"Stay away from my mommy and me!"* That was it, the clerk never bothered me again. Roxie was like this everywhere.

If someone did not make a good first impression on her,

she would just bark at them to stay away from her and me. She wouldn't even let them come near me. She was very protective of me. Roxie even saved my life once. It was at the time when a Valero Gas Station was robbed. I had an appointment, and after I was done with it, I stopped at Valero Gas station, as I was running low on gas. It was not the same station that was robbed, but a different one. I got out of the car to fill the tank. While I was filling the tank, I saw a white van roll into the lane, next to mine and a man got out. He started approaching me. I asked him to stop, but he did not listen or even respond to my request. I asked him nicely that he should stay away from the car, and not get near it. However, he did not listen and kept approaching. Roxie who was in the driver's seat once again sensed my distress and started growling at the man in a very threatening manner.

When he heard Roxie, the man stopped. Roxie then started barking loudly, and in a very threatening manner. The man started backing away. Roxie took one leap across to the passenger side window that was nearer to the man. The man completely backed off and went to the van, saying to the driver that the lady had a vicious dog with her. Even though Roxie was not a vicious dog, she was very protective of me. I was glad that I had her in my life.

Who knows what might have happened that afternoon at the gas station. I am certain that the man was a robber and had come with the intention of mugging me. However, I cannot be sure about that, just glad that I had Roxie with me. Roxie had a lot of quirks that I have never seen in other dogs all my life. She was unique and did things her own way. She would never be bullied into liking something. Not even treats or food would motivate her to do something she did not like. She was the most curious dog I had known. Roxie was always ready to try anything new. Once, even though she did not like baths, she jumped into a lake just because she thought it looked fun. However, it turned out to be the opposite of that for poor Roxie, as the water was ice cold. Since she was a quick learner, after that one incident, she was always careful to check the temperature of the water before jumping in. If it was not possible for her to dip her paw into the water to test its temperature, she would remain on dry land and not go in at all. She had to verify it for herself.

Roxie never liked it when I left her alone at the house, and would start to get anxious. Then to show me that she did not like it that I had left her alone, she would tear up a pillow or scratch at the entrance door, until the paint was peeling from it. It was her way of punishing me for leaving her alone. Even though she was more patient while she waited for me in the car, if I was late coming back to the car, she would have done something like gnaw on the car seat cover, the seat belt, or even her own leash. It was such a human gesture that I was always taken in by her behavior, and it never made me angry. I would try not to leave her in the car for long as well. For she was a sweetheart and would wait for me patiently for quite some time. She only chewed on the seat belt and her leash, if I took a really long time; which only happened rarely to begin with, so it was not a big problem. I took care of it and so Roxie and I did not have any problems with that, after it happened a couple of times. Another thing Roxie did that made me think that she was at least part human, was the way she would look at the people who sat in the passenger seat.

It was always a very watchful look that said, *"Remember I am back here, and I am keeping an eye on you, so mind you no funny business."* I would always be surprised when she would bark at the exact right times. If someone was touching the radio, for example, she would bark at them knowing that I did not like it, if someone changed it to any channel other than my favorite. It was also Roxie's favorite channel, so she was twice as much invested in making the person not change the channel. It was like that with everyone who sat in the passenger seat. It was Roxie in front when no one else rode with us. However, if we had company, Roxie would ride in the back seat, so she would keep an eye on things from her vantage point.

Roxie was also very protective of the car. She would not let anyone near it, and she would bark loudly at them until they backed away. If they did not, she would bump her nose against the window to show that the moment they opened the door, she would jump on them. She knew how to scare people. Even though she was not an aggressive dog and did not normally bite people, I knew she would bite them if they crossed her. If people kept coming at her while she was barking, it was at their own peril. She was warning them, and so would I, if anyone approached her while I was there, and she would bark, I would tell them to back off. If they did not then, it was their fault that they got hurt.

She was protective and quirky, but she was also a brat sometimes, as I have earlier described. She hated it if I left her alone for an extended period of time. Once she chewed up my friend's jacket in protest of me leaving her in the car, while I stopped and got out to say hi to her. I had to buy a new jacket for her. My crazy mutt would sometimes give me a hard time, but she loved me very much and would show it to me throughout the day, by doing little things for me. So, I loved her even when she was acting out a little. It was nothing a human would not do, and a human would never be able to make me as happy as Roxie made me, throughout the time she was with me.

Chapter 6
Strangers

    I am extremely sure that Roxie was an above-average, intelligent dog. I have never met any dog before her nor after her, who had any habit that was quite like her habits. Yes, she did a lot of things that most dogs would do, but there were just a few things that were totally unique to her. Like I have already mentioned that she was very attached to me, and would seriously go crazy if I left her alone for any length of time. She never took a liking to strangers straight away, and I had to train her as a puppy not to jump on people when she saw them, while on her walks. It was a funny incident, when my father was over at my condo, and decided to take Roxie for a walk. She was still very young, around seven months old, and I had at this time, not fully trained her.

My dad took her for a walk by the lagoon, but when he came back, he was not very pleased as Roxie had spent most of the walk jumping up on people. It was something she really enjoyed doing as a puppy. My dad told me that this dog is not trained, and he never took her for a walk again. Although my dad liked dogs, he was a little impatient and did not understand that some puppies required more effort than others.

Roxie was among the puppies that required constant attention. She would get mad at me if I left her alone, and shred anything she could get her teeth and paws on. It was more often than not, her own bed or a couch pillow. The incident with my sister when I accidentally left Roxie alone for longer than I expected, was the final straw for her. She had scratched up the door and torn quite a few pillows, and after that, the anxiety had definitely doubled.

She would greet me with such enthusiasm when I got back from getting the mail. Judging by her barks and jumps, it would seem like I had been out for hours and not just a few minutes. Her tail would be wagging a mile a minute, and would not stop for a long time. Even though it was a source of slight jealousy, I was always glad that Roxie got along really well with her sitter.

The reason I say that I am jealous, is that sometimes I thought she liked her better than me, because she would always get a lot more excited when she would join the two of us for a walk. However, Roxie would put all my fears to rest, as soon as I started getting these thoughts. It was like she would understand that I was beginning to feel jealous, and she would immediately come and lick my hand, or do something to get my attention so that I was reassured.

She would always do cute little things like this, which would help me let go of all the doubts that Roxie loved her sitter more than she loved me. Like the time when we went to visit Mount Tallac, and I had injured my knee. Roxie knew that I was hurt and she was keen to look after me. Every now and then, she would walk beside me slowly and caress my hand with her nose or her forehead, as if she were encouraging me to keep going.

Her expressions would almost communicate the words, *"Mom you are going to be okay, just walk slowly, I am right here beside you"* This was something that was dear to me, her companionship. She was a comforting as well an entertaining part of my life that I just miss so much sometimes. Her ways were unique and complex like I have already stated; sometimes it felt as if I was living with another person.

For a dog, she was good at communicating her wishes as well. By her responses, I knew that she liked the butterfly patterned scarf that I got for her. She would get so happy and would jump around to show that she was pleased with my choice. She also loved to get gifts. Many times I would come back home she would come to greet me at the door, and jump up and down and smell my hands as if she was asking me, *"What did you get for me mom?"*

This habit of hers was so adorable that I usually got her something when I came back, usually a treat for her to eat. She was never without her treats. I would always keep them on hand, because she was such a picky eater. She would hardly ever eat her meal in one sitting. Another thing that Roxie did that I found really adorable was posing for photographs. She would just understand that she had to stay still and not move around, while I was taking a picture of her. She was a photogenic dog who knew how to pose for photographs. I really liked taking her pictures, especially when we went for our morning walks. Roxie was the epitome of a crazy mutt. Crazy Mutt, yes that was my nickname for her. She would do the most random things, and act as if it was all normal.

One of the reasons I started calling her a crazy mutt, was that she was not very fond of strangers. As I have mentioned, I had to train her not to jump up on people, when she was just a little puppy. So, even though she understood that jumping on people was a no-no, she never got over her dislike of strangers. The incident with the man at the grocery store where she barked at him for tapping on the window to get her attention, was just one among many such incidents.

When I left her alone in the car, she would not let any stranger approach. She would bark at them and show her teeth, as if to say, *"One step closer and I will bite you."* Although she never did bite or injure anyone, she was not immediately friendly with strangers. She liked to take her time getting to know them, and even then, she would rely on her first impression of the person. If she really disliked someone at first sight, she would not change her opinion very often. Once around 2004, when Roxie was about 2 years old, I had a date with a guy, and he came over to my place. I thought of him as a good person. The best thing was that he liked dogs; that was one of the reasons that I liked him and invited him over. However, when he came over, he did not get along with Roxie at all. Even though he was trying, Roxie did not respond to him at all.

She just stood there and looked at him, and then turned away. He seemed put off, so I told him that Roxie took a little time getting warm around strange people, and she did not like to share in my affection with anyone else. At first, he seemed satisfied with the explanation, and after that little incident, we both had dinner. Dinner went by without any mention of Roxie not even responding, when he tried to give her treats from his plate.

Although, I did see him making faces at her. After dinner, the two of us thought it would be a good idea if we stayed in and watched a movie on the couch, rather than go out. So we settled down on the couch and started a movie.

We were only a few minutes into the movie, when Roxie thought that it would be a good idea to come in and settle down between the two of us. I, of course, did not mind, but my date tried to move Roxie off to the side.

It was a little bit comic at first as he would move Roxie off to the side, and she would just get down from the couch, take a walk around the room, come back and jump in between us again. This went on for about half an hour, and by now he was starting to get angry with her behavior. I tried to tell him that she was a dog and even though she was smarter than other dogs, she was still a dog. If she wanted to sit between us, it was of no consequence.

We were, after all, just only watching a movie. To be honest, it was only the first date. I initially liked the guy a lot. However, by the time he was on the couch with me, he had removed Roxie from between us quite a few times. Seeing this, I was starting to have second thoughts about him. I was starting to think that Roxie had the correct idea about him right from the start.

She did not like him from the moment she met him. Getting between us on the couch was her way of looking after me. She wanted me to be careful what kind of men I let into the house, and I thought to myself that from now on, I was going to be very careful who I invite into the home. Especially for the men I would date in the future, I was going to get them verified from Roxie first. That girl had a good nose, picking out the wrong men.

She was not very polite to the grocery store guy, and he was kind of a jerk, coming up to the window and tapping on it. I thought it was rude, and Roxie thought so as well, so she kept barking at him. She did not like it when people did that; knock on the window, when she was inside the car. The thing with Roxie was that she hated loud noises. Whenever the fire alarm would go off, it would drive her crazy, and she would drive me crazy in return until I got it fixed.

She was one of the pickiest dogs I have ever known, but for all her pickiness she is also the most loving dog, to have come into my life. She taught me patience and love, as well as generosity and kindness. She also made me have a lot of fun too. Anyways, after that night, I would always get Roxie's approval before I let a guy come into the house on a date.

Even though the guy said that he liked animals, he did

not understand how to get along with Roxie, and he was taking offense on the tiniest of things. Suddenly, he was not that good anymore, and I never invited him back. I read somewhere that whippets or whippet mix dogs get really attached to their owners, and that was very true of Roxie. She was attached to me and did not like it, when I went away from her for very long.

One more thing that Roxie liked to do that whippets or whippet mix was known for was hogging the furniture. Roxie really liked to stretch out on my couch, in front to the TV. She would jump straight up onto it, right after she got home from a walk and I had cleaned her up. She knew after only a few months of training that it was not okay to jump up onto the couch, if she was dirty or dusty. I kept telling my dad that Roxie was a very trainable dog, you just had to take your time and be patient with her, and she would learn anything.

She learned so many tricks that she used to perform in senior homes. I also read that Whippets were not barkers, but Roxie used to bark a lot, especially if people came to my condo or even if they were passing by outside. She would always give them warning kind of barks. She did not want people to come in, and her barks would always give a warning that someone was approaching.

I liked that, I guess it was the other part of her breed that was showing up, the Vizsla, whenever she barked. Even though I liked it when she gave me a warning that someone was approaching, I did not like it when she would go into my spare room, jump up on the twin bed, look out the window, and bark at total strangers who were just passing by. It was her favorite pastime. Anytime she caught the room door open, she would just dart inside, jump up on the bed, and start barking away. It was that continuous barking that made me call her a *"crazy mutt,"* take her out of that room, and keep the door firmly closed. When Roxie got older, it was then she learned not to go into the room and bark at people when looking out the window.

Roxie was a docile and playful dog who was always ready to have fun. She loved to go to the Banana Store, which is a music store near where I live. She loved to go there, and they loved to have her there. She would have a lot of fun with them, and they, in turn, would enjoy her company as well. That was the one place she liked going to.

Another time, I took Roxie to a Subway restaurant and

told her to wait outside, while I went in to get a drink for myself and water for Roxie. I sat her down by one of the tables that were arranged outside, and I did not even tie her leash. I knew she would not wander off and would stay where I left her. However, it was a little crowded in there, and it took me around 15 minutes to get to the cash register.

As I was purchasing the water, Roxie who was tired of waiting and had already sat for 15 minutes waiting for me to come out, came into the shop to check up on me. Everyone there paused what they were doing, to look at the dog who had just wandered in. I looked at her and told her to wait outside, as I was just about to pay the cashier and come out. Roxie wagged her tail and went right back outside to wait for me.

The cashier was really surprised and looked at me, I told him that the water was for the dog who had just come in, as she was my dog. Not only did the cashier attend to me immediately, but also commented that he had never seen a more well-behaved dog. He said that the way Roxie responded to me was as if she was actually understanding what I was telling her to do.

Sure enough, when I went outside with my drink and water for her, she was patiently sitting by the exact same table that I had left her by. I really loved it when Roxie listened to me and did what I told her to, and sometimes I even liked it when she did what she wanted, regardless of what I told her. Like in the case of my date, Roxie did what she wanted regardless of what I told her, and it saved me from a relationship with a guy who was not at all right for me. My relationship with Roxie was as complex as any relationship between two human beings, and she was just a dog. This is among the reasons that I miss her so much. She was just the kind of dog who would grow on the hearts of people, who were just like her. The kind and gentle ones; the patient ones; and the generous and compassionate ones.

She made my circle of friends better, by getting me to include people in my life who had more of these qualities. It is because of these people in my life that I will always remember Roxie; the crazy mutt who came into my life and made it so much better. She even changed my nature too. She taught me how to be patient with her. The reason I keep repeating this, is because Roxie would never learn anything until it was shown to her personally.

Like, for example, the thing where she used to go into my spare room and jump on the twin bed and bark at random passersby. Well, that was something that drove me a little crazy, so I was a little impatient with her when I told her not to go into that room. She did not listen until and unless a few months later, when I had started getting over my irritation and had learned to say it to her with patience. I think she did it to make me a better person.

It was as if she wanted to say, *"Mommy, you know I love you and would listen to you, but you should not get so upset over this."* With time I learned that she was right. There was no use getting upset over this. What really mattered was the time that we spent with each other. And it was a good time that we spent together. It was happy and comforting for both of us.

Chapter 7
Garbage Dog

While Roxie was a perfect, sweet dog, she did not it like when strangers came to her and petted her. It was like she was thinking to herself, *"Do I know this person?"*

"Why is that man petting me?"

"What do you want?"

"Do I know you from somewhere?"

"I don't think we have met before, so please stop petting me." Every time anyone took the liberty of getting to know Roxie, she would respond with dignity most of the time,

but if you crossed the limits of her patience, that was when Roxie would get angry. She was a kind of dog who wasn't shy of standing up for herself. She demonstrated her patience when I went to a supermarket, and left her in the car for a bit. It was only a little while when I went in and grabbed a few things.

When I came back, I had a shop assistant accompany me to help me carry my purchases to the car. When he saw Roxie inside, just like most other people, he also wanted to get her attention, so he started tapping on the car's window. To me, it seems a little rude when anyone just does that without permission. Although I knew his intentions were not wrong, and he just wanted to say *hi* to the dog.

But you cannot explain these distinctions to the dog. So, I introduced him to Roxie while she continued to ignore the man. I said to the guy, *"If you want to say hi to her, you can go stand by the entrance and I will bring her by. She doesn't respond well to strangers introducing themselves."*

After that, I took Roxie out and did what I had told the guy I would do, but as I proceeded to walk Roxie past him, she completely ignored him, as she had been in the car. For me, that was a surprise considering she was a very forgiving dog. I guess if you crossed limits, she was not willing to forgive. The clerk had been a bit rude, in assuming that she wanted to respond at that moment. I think tapping the window was what she had taken offense at. To me, it was all good. I did not want her to behave like I wanted her to. She had her own personality and her own character. She was going to be who she wanted to be, and I was going to let her do what she wanted.

The reason I am saying this is that I have seen many people trying to train their dogs to behave a certain way, when that is not in their nature. Dog training can extend to tricks and going to the bathroom, but how to react to people is not something we should force upon them. There are a few dogs who naturally like being outgoing, and take very well with strangers. But that is not how my Roxie was.

She was a little reserved, and was not fond of being petted by everyone, especially not on the head. If she thought they really wanted to pet her, she would turn around, and offer her back rump to them, so that they could pet her to their heart's content. She would even dance a little, when people petted her on her rump. I was happy with who she was. She sometimes used to drive me crazy, but even then, I loved her with all my heart.

She was never far from me, and always liked to stick close to me. She would get really upset with me if I left her even for a little while, and that was something I did not like doing anyway. The reason I think she got upset over me going anywhere without her was, partly anxiety, and partly her desire to protect me. She loved showing everyone that she was my protector. She would bark and didn't stop, when anyone approached my condo.

I had to tell her to stop, only then she would stop barking. Even then, if she didn't like the person who had come over, she would continue to growl every now and then, to make sure they remembered that she was there, keeping a watchful eye on them. Like I have said, Roxie was not someone who took a liking to people at the first meeting, yet there were a few exceptions.

Like her sitter, for example, she was totally in love with her, and she had been one of the few rare people who Roxie had taken a liking to, at the very first sight. That was the first time that had happened in front of me, and I was surprised that Roxie could do that. I mean, before then, I had just assumed that Roxie would never be the kind of dog, who instantly took a liking to people, but there she was, liking Laura on the first go.

I was happy that she was capable of liking people and her choice was good. Laura was a really good person, and I was happy to get to know her more. Roxie was the reason Laura came into our lives. I had hired her initially to be a walker for Roxie, and then when I found that Roxie really liked her, I asked her to be a sitter for Roxie as well. It worked out really well, since I would leave Roxie with Laura especially, if I had to work the night shift at Guide Dogs.

I liked it when Roxie would ignore a stranger, who would come to her and try to pet her, or talk to her. Her expressions were really funny to me. It was hilarious watching people get flustered by her lack of reaction. It was like when you start tickling one of your friends, only to discover that they are immune to it. It is an awkward situation, and that was what happened with Roxie and the strangers who came to talk to her.

She would literally not give them any response. However, there was one time when she did the totally unexpected. I was at a grocery store and had left her in the car for a while. When I came back, I started loading the things I had purchased into my car, when a couple of boys came into the parking lot. They approached the car, and I think they were going to pass by me, but then they saw Roxie in the front passenger seat and began to approach the car. I told them to stay away and not to get too near my car. They, however, just ignored me and kept on coming toward the car. I even told them that Roxie was a guard dog and that I could set her loose on them, if they continued to approach. It was by this time that Roxie guessed what I was saying, and that I did not want these youngsters approaching my car.

She was standing at the passenger window facing the approaching boys. Suddenly, she bared her teeth and let out a long, threatening growl. Then, she jumped forward as if she was going to break the window of the car and be at these guys' throats. Even though I knew that she had never even bitten anyone in her life, I was glad that she caught on to the fact that I did not want those boys anywhere near me, and acted accordingly.

Roxie was really great at catching on to my thoughts this way. I was really pleased with her that day. She had done something that I did not even think was possible for her. It was after that incident that I stopped believing, there was anything she could not do. If the situation was dire enough and required her doing something, and it was within the scope of her capabilities, she would get the job done. She had pretended to be a guard dog when the situation had required it of her. Her acting skills were amazing that day. For a moment, I thought that she, for some reason, had gotten furious and was really going to break the window. However, once those boys had run away, Roxie returned to being cool as a cucumber, and acted as if she had just gotten up to change her position on the passenger seat, and went back to being seated on it.

She was that calm! Afterward, when I recounted this incident to Laura, her sitter, and my sister, Roxie stood staring at us looking pleased with herself, her tail wagging a dozen times a minute, and her tongue hanging out of her mouth making it look like she was grinning at us saying, *"I did well, didn't I mommy? I scared those boys away just like that!"*

Roxie was a force of nature and brought happiness to my life, as no one else had done. She made sure that I was okay if I got hurt and she would try to keep people away from me, who she thought were not good enough for me - like the guy I was dating who kept getting jealous of Roxie sitting between us, while we watched the movie. I still get so surprised when I think about it.

That was some really bizarre thinking on that guy's part. What was really surprising was that Roxie already had an inkling that he wasn't the right guy for me, and the way she proceeded to tell me exactly how he was not really the guy for me. I was really happy with the way she handled that situation. Even though Roxie was not fond of strangers, when I taught her to perform her trick, she would love to get in front of people, and perform for them.

She was not that shy of a dog, and at such times, she did not mind that people come to her and try to pet her. She would understand that people were admiring her for performing such wonderful tricks. Even then she would not let them pet her head, but rather her rump only.

She would be pleased when she offered her rump to be petted, people would laugh and admire her even more, and that would make her do a little dance of pleasure, which would attract even more admiration from the crowd. She loved attention, and that is why she was such a great performer.

Roxie also loved getting treats, and after every trick, she would look to me like, *"Okay now I know I did that good, mommy, treat time please."* Roxie looked adorable with her tongue hanging out, waiting for her beloved treats. Even though she was not really a big eater, she loved her treats. I guess they gave her a sense of accomplishment that she had performed her tricks well, and that is why she was being rewarded.

I noticed this when she was learning a trick, she would not ask for treats that often, preferring to keep practicing until she had gotten it down. Then, she would ask for treats every time she did it perfectly. That was one of the reasons, why I would not say no to treats all that often. She was already a picky eater, and now that she was looking forward to eating even her treats, I was not going to say no to that.

Even though Roxie was not food-motivated, I did catch her going through my kitchen trash quite a few times. She just loved to rummage in the kitchen garbage. I even caught her going through my father's kitchen trash once, while we were at his house. She snuck back into the kitchen and tried to get into the garbage can, while my attention was diverted. She just did the darnedest things.

I would get her good food to eat that was really highly rated for dogs, but that mutt preferred going through the garbage herself. She was not very fond of wet food. If anything I got her was wet or soupy, she simply would not touch it. The best thing she liked to eat was a piece of my bagel that I had brought from a café, and every time I got it, she would look at me as if asking me if she could get a piece right away.

Her expressions were always so adorable that I could never say no to her, and always ended up sharing half my bagel with her. Like I have already said many times in this book, and will likely be telling a few more time before this ends, I loved Roxie with all my heart and soul. She brought the brightest and the happiest time of my life. She made me feel like I was living with an actual person.

She was a complicated mess of emotions, and I just loved her expressions. I had almost no difficulty, deciphering them and making sense of what she was trying to tell me. She was also very understanding of me. I would ask Roxie to do something, and she would do it. Like when she was sitting on the couch, and I would ask her to get off it, since I had just cleaned it she would obey but with a facial expression that said, *"Oh okay, mommy, getting off, but I am also clean, you are the one who washed me."* These expressions of Roxie usually made me laugh. They were somehow so eloquent. Anyways, she even understood that she had to stay put, and wait for me when I asked her to, and would very rarely not listen to me. There was only one time I remember that she left the car, while I left her in it. She never did it before that time and afterward either. I would leave the car windows open for her, knowing that she was not going to jump out and go wandering about. However, she did jump out of the car once, when I had parked it to go into a store with my sister. When both of us got back, Roxie was not in the car. She was nearby on the pavement, but I was not able to figure out why she had gotten out.

First, when I saw that the car was empty, I thought that maybe someone had taken her, but that was very unlikely. Roxie would not go with anyone, without barking a lot and drawing a lot of attention. My next thought was that she had jumped out and gotten on the road, but that possibility I did not even bear thinking about. Before I could panic a lot, both my sister and I saw Roxie standing by the pavement and ran to her. I asked her to explain to me why she jumped out of the car, but Roxie was a dog after all, and to this day I do not know why she jumped out.

However, my sister and I came to the conclusion that someone must have tried to pet her, or annoyed her somehow for her to leave the car. But she was true to her protective nature even then. She had not wandered far from the car, and was still standing as a guard dog near it. She knew that the windows were open and that it was not somehow secure enough for her, to leave the car and look to find me. She stayed where she was, waiting for me to return.

That was the way with Roxie. She almost always thought things through, especially as she got older. She was impulsive when she was a puppy but as a grownup, being cautious was also an important part of her nature. I miss her a lot, and she will always be a part of me.

My Dog is my Heart.

Chapter 8
Friend

Dogs are said to be man's best friend. They are also known to be amongst the most social animals on the earth, apart from humans. So, it was only a matter of time before Roxie made a few more friends herself, other than me. She was a very social dog, who was also wary of people. As I said, she was as complex as a human. She had a mixture of traits. While she loved to hang out with a few people, she did not allow a few others to even come near her, let alone pet her. She was very particular about her choice, when finding companions for her play. That is how she chose her sitter. She became immediately fond of her, and I was glad since it made it so much easier in my mind that I was leaving Roxie with someone who treated her well, and whom Roxie liked very much.

There were some people whom Roxie disliked, like there was a guy who had come over to my house for a date as I have described. I liked him, but Roxie was not so polite with him, and took an immediate dislike toward him. It turned out that she was right in judging him. He was not as big an animal lover as he had claimed to be. So I was not so interested in him. Roxie saved me that time from a relationship that would have started, based on a lie, had she not intervened. She was always on the lookout for the people she cared.

Roxie was no ordinary dog. She was smart in every way and a challenge that kept me on my toes. When I took her to work for the first time, she immediately became everyone's favorite. However, she would not let people pet her. If anyone approached her, she would turn her back to them and have them pet her behind, and each time someone did that, she would do a little dance for them. That little antic of her kept my colleagues laughing for the whole of that day. Another one of her hits were the tricks that Roxie performed for the elderly, in retirement homes. She loved to do that and liked the appreciation and admiration everyone showered her with, at the end of each one of her shows. She looked forward to the treats, as well as praises from the audience. Even though she was not very food-oriented, she loved to get treats.

She would always look up to me with her tongue out, whenever she finished one of her tricks successfully. I loved giving her treats but had to be careful. Otherwise, she would get so full of them that she would not eat her dinner, and then spoil her whole eating schedule. That was one thing I had to be very careful about - her eating. She was a picky eater ever since she was a little puppy.

Roxie loved to make new friends when she wanted. She was a caring dog, who would look after anyone she thought needed her help. There was a dog we took care of. She was a retired breeder from Guide Dogs, named Natoma. She was a yellow Labrador who loved to follow Roxie. Roxie, in fact, told Natoma off once, when she tried to jump on an elderly person. Roxie was smart enough to know that it was a huge no-no and stopped Natoma just in time, by getting between her and the person; all the while barking at Natoma in an insistent and chiding manner. It was a bark that translated well into a chastising sort of bark.

It was like she was saying, *"Don't do that, Natoma. It is not a polite way to behave."*

One time, Natoma was watching Roxie do hoop jumping and decided to try it. After a few tries, she got the hang of it and spent the rest of the afternoon trying it, until she perfected it. She seemed to enjoy doing it. After she went back to her breeder, she even showed off her new skill to him. Whenever I took care of Natoma after that, she came with Roxie and me, and I took her with me to some of the shows at retirement homes, until she passed away at the age of 12.

Roxie continued to perform at retirement homes for another seven years, until I retired her as well, when she was almost nine years old. She told me she did not want to do the tricks anymore. She just wanted to be my girl. As I have shared earlier, she had hurt herself during a show jumping through a hoop, and did not want to do any more hard tricks. This is what did her in. It was because of her injury that I retired her at nine. Even though she could have done it for a few more years, as she indeed was energetic enough for it. However, she was tired of doing the same thing over and over again. I think she wanted to try her hand at something different. However, she continued to perform the tricks she had learned very well, and still put on her 'shows' for the family members, whenever they were over at the house and requested it.

Before Guide Dogs made a rule that employees could not take any active dog home, Roxie and I took care of another breeder and Felix's guide, Ned. Roxie loved them and played with them. She enjoyed the company they provided, which was a rare occurrence for her. She had a hard time making friends, whether it was humans or dogs. In the case of most dogs, including Natoma, they would chase cats.

However, Roxie was unique in this regard. She never chased a cat in her life. If she ever had a chance of meeting a cat, she would just go up to them and sniff them for a while, that too, if they let her. Otherwise, she would leave the cats well alone. However, squirrels were a different story. Roxie hated squirrels. They would tease her and then run away from her, almost as if daring her to chase them. It was almost a playful, sibling kind of a relationship that Roxie had with them. They would come up to her and tease, and then when she managed to get free for a while to run around the park, she would chase them until they would run up the tree, after which she would come to either sit with me or continue the walk. She would resume whatever she had been doing before the chase had begun, as though she was not even interrupted by them.

I always found her demeanor after the squirrel chases funny. Roxie would assume the air of nonchalance, as though nothing had ever happened. I think it was because she very rarely managed to catch the squirrels, as they were always wily and more fast-footed than her. There was one incident with a cat that teased Roxie, and then ran and hid under my car. Roxie ran after her.

I thought it was finally going to begin an era of chasing a cat. However, Roxie just went to the car, put her head under it, and gave one loud bark. That was all it took for the cat to yowl and scatter. She never bothered Roxie again. Among the several things that were unique about Roxie, the best thing I like now when she has gone far away from me, is that she was extremely photogenic. All the pictures that I took of her, came out looking great.

Another unique thing about her was that she loved posing for photos, and knew that she had to sit still for them to come out good. What a character she was! I took some photographs of her, doing the cutest things. If she knew I was photographing, she would try to do new poses for me and get my attention, if I looked away for even a second by giving cute little barks, as though she was saying, *"Look, mommy, new pose, take a picture quickly."*

Her expressions were sometimes funny, when I photographed her like she was being goofy on purpose. One of the photographs was at the Art and Garden Center located in Ross Calif. It was right after someone's wedding, and there was a glass of wine and some rose petals in a basket. I put the glass of wine and rose petals on the stage, and had Roxie sit by them. She looked down at the glass of wine.

The look she gave me after taking a sniff of the glass was, *"Mom that stuff smells so bad, yuck!"*

Then, Roxie turned her head away from it, as I snapped the photograph. That was one of the best images I took of her. It was the most expressive one, in fact. I put it into a calendar a few years ago, with some other photographs of her.

Roxie was a big teaser, whenever she wanted to be. On a nice grassy area when I would let her lose, she would run with full speed in circles, and make you chase her. Then she would stop in a playful mood, and run in the opposite direction with full speed. When she got tired, she would come back to me, and we would continue our walk.

She did the same thing with Laura, who was her sitter and took care of her while I was at work. Laura told me that

Roxie was one funny dog, and that she was very smart as well. One of the tricks that I did use too often, was that I would tell Roxie to say the word *'Buffalo'* and Roxie, being Roxie, would try and it would almost sound like she was saying it, *'Ruffalo.'* One of the things that she did not like, in particular, was taking a bath. She did not like getting into the water. Whenever I would give her a bath, she would jump out multiple times. Even though it happened less, as she grew up, she was not at all comfortable taking baths. She was very much like a cat in this regard. In fact, whenever she did something bad, I would punish her by sending her to a bath. It got to the point where she would herself go and get into the bathtub, if she did something terrible and knew it. Roxie was sweet and docile, and playful at most times.

Whenever I took her to Bananas at Large, a music store, people there loved playing with her. She showed them her playful mood and loved going there. She liked going to places where people would appreciate her, and not just come up to her to pet her. She liked to interact with people in a meaningful way. That is why Bananas at Large was a place she loved to hang out at. She even enjoyed the soft, background music playing there. Even though she did not appreciate loud and irritating noises, she liked to listen to soft music sometimes.

The last time I took her there, she was about 14 years old, not as playful when she was younger, yet she enjoyed her visit thoroughly. There was a time I remember when I took Roxie to my sister's place during vacations. The whole family was there including my brother, his wife, and my cute little nephew who had just turned four. Roxie was having the time of her life, running around the place. She especially loved the fact that my sister's kitchen had two entry doors. She would get my nephew to chase her in one door and out the other. Soon, the two of them were running after each other and playing a spirited game of tag.

Roxie loved to play with my nephew, whenever she got the chance. She loved him a lot and played with him gently, making him laugh and giggle with her antics. She liked to watch over him and would never let him fall, running and catching him before he could fall. There were times, however, when I had to stop them, and get her to behave herself. What a crazy mutt, having fun with a four years old playing with her! But I would not do that very often, as she played gently with him.

Even though Roxie was good friends with many dogs, like Natoma and Ned, she did not like all dogs. She was attacked by several dogs twice. Once, when she was walking with me, a neighbor's dog attacked her without warning. She was shocked that another dog would behave like that. After that, she became cautious whenever she saw another dog.

Another incident was while my garage was being fixed, I had to walk her down the stairs, and pass this condo that had a dog barking and hitting the screen door. When I saw that, it bothered Roxie a lot. I asked the owner very politely, to please close her door. But she did not listen to me, and the next time I had to walk by her condo, her dog broke through the screen door and attacked Roxie, without any provocation from Roxie's side.

The lady then came out, got her dog, dragged him inside, and closed the door. Ever since this second incident of an unprovoked attack, Roxie would hide behind me, whenever a dog rushed up to her, as she did not have an idea if the dog was friendly or not. Roxie had an outgoing personality, and she would like it very much when people treated her well and admired her for her qualities.

She liked to be a caretaker, as well as get loved by people, when they took care of her in return. She would be elated when I brought little gifts for her. She especially liked scarves. I loved her complex personality very much. And like I have already said, it seemed to me that I was living with another person, and not a pet when she was around. I would always be surprised by her response. She always kept me on her toes - that adorable mutt.

Chapter 9
That Crazy Mutt

Roxie was a study of a lifetime, and try as I might, I cannot fully explain how much of a crazy mutt she was. She was the dearest to me, and from time to time, I still think about her running around with other dogs up in heaven, having her treats and teaching other dogs how to behave.

She liked to show her skills off, and that included manners as well. Ever since she was a puppy, even in the briefest time she had with her sister, she was the one who used to understand instructions first and then convey them to her. I always found this trait of Roxie's, very endearing. She did the same with Natoma as well. Roxie was usually a level-headed dog, but she did have her moments of craziness as well.

When she would get into a playful mood, she would rouse everyone around her, and invite them to join her in doing crazy things. For example, she loved to forage in the kitchen dumpster. Once, I took her to my dad's house. While all of us were sitting in the living room talking and I was distracted from her antics for a bit, she sneaked into the kitchen and proceeded to paw at it, as if looking for something to eat; even though she had just been fed and had refused to eat more.

I think she enjoyed hunting for her food, as a kind of reward for all the hard work involved in the process. She used to do the same thing even at our house, due to which I had learned to keep my wastebasket out of her way, and had to do the same at my dad's house for the remainder of the evening. I was not opposed to giving Roxie treats, especially if she had been more peckish than usual because of her food in the evenings, but I did prefer that she had a proper dinner, so that she got proper nutrition. She loved to sit by me and watch me eat, always hoping for tidbits. I taught her early on, never to beg for food scraps at the table. I taught her to patiently wait for me to finish my food, and then whatever was left on my plate, I would put in her bowl, and she would eagerly gobble it up.

Being Roxie, she was a mixture of both patience and impatience. She would wait for me to finish up, but she would also be impatient to get a bit of my food, especially if we were eating out. She really loved to go to San Rafael restaurant with me, and sit outside while I fed her a piece of my lunch. Roxie was an energetic dog who did not get sick very often.

She loved running a lot and would find excuses to go out for walks. As I said, she was a well-behaved dog most of the time, and never chased animals on her walks in the park unless I let her. However, running up and down stairs was something that she enjoyed more. One place that she loved zooming downstairs, was at her favorite store,

Bananas at Large. I suspect that was also one of the reasons, she was in love with that store.

Even though being nice and polite was prevalent in her nature, Roxie could be a brat sometimes, and when she was, she turned everything upside down. She especially did not like it, if I locked her up. It did not matter where it was that I was locking her up. Just the fact that she was locked up made her mad. Once, I took her to my sister's house and because she was being too rowdy, I locked her in a room upstairs for a while.

When I went back to check on her, she had torn up some pillows, and as soon as I had the door opened, she tore out of the room and ran down the stairs and ran straight into a wall. I had to go and pick her up bodily. Thank God, she did not hurt herself. After that, she began to hate that room, and anytime we went over to my sister's place, she would stay clear of that room.

Another time, I left Roxie at my house to go over to my sister's house for a party. I believed that she was well fed and taken care of. I did not worry about anything as she was already housebroken, and just in case she got a little hungry, I had left some treats for her. I had anticipated that

I would not be gone for a long time, only two or three hours at the most. However, it took me quite some time to get back, and by then, all her patience had been tried, and its limits had long been crossed. So, she had torn the place up and was in the process of scratching my door raw. In fact, I believe that if I had been just another hour late, she would have managed to break the door down. It was the only time I left Roxie alone for long. I understood that she could cope with separation and being left alone. However, there were a few other instances where I had to lock her up, even if it was for a little time, like the time I took her to work.

When I first brought her to GDB, I tied her. However, that was not a very successful plan. Every time someone walked into the office, she would bark at them, and no matter what I would do to get her to quiet down, she would only listen to me for one time. Whenever another person would step in, she would be at it again. Even though she was a nicely behaved dog, she did not like being with strangers.

So the poor girl had to go into a kennel outside of my office. Kennel number 4 was assigned to her, and she stayed there until lunchtime. Dana, one of my co-workers, and I put a wooden doghouse there for her with a blanket.

That mutt hated being locked up so much that she chewed the doghouse, and we had to replace it with a lagoon, made of hard plastic. She even started to chew that as well. However, once I sprayed it with some bitter stuff, she stopped chewing it. She did not like it at all, and the good thing was that she stopped chewing it. One of her favorite things to do on a cold night when Roxie was young, was to get into the bed with me and crawl under the covers right next to me with her favorite toy, and cuddle with me for warmth. Since whippets have short coats, they get cold far more easily than other dogs.

Talking about her toys, if they squeaked, she would chew on them until she would get the squeaker out and play with it. It always scared me that she would swallow it, but being an above intelligent dog, she never did. Apart from my bed, the other place she loved to lay on, was my couch, especially when I was out. Sometimes, when I got home, she would be lying on my couch.

As she got old, I had to put chairs on the couch so she would not get on them, since getting off the couch without a stool, was painful for her aching shoulder and back. Roxie was a perfect show dog. Even though I was the only one who trained her, she was exemplary as she delivered every trick that I had taught her perfectly. She was perfect on stage as well, as she loved attention. She loved it in every form, be it live at the shows she did, or in the form of I taking her pictures. One time, she did an entertainment at Guide Dogs for the Blind Fun Day, about nine years ago on stage. What a show off she was! She knew that she had done a good job on the stage, and when I was taking her pictures, she posed for me by staying still until I took the pictures. She loved making people laugh and have a good time.

Even after she got hurt doing the trick at nine years of age, she continued to perform at family and friends gatherings, whenever people encouraged her. Running was, by far, one of Roxie's favorite hobbies. When she was young, she would run up the stairs, in front of my condo with full speed. She would wait for me at the top, and then we would continue our long hike down to Bon Air shopping center, and after that over to the lagoon, finally coming back home.

It was during one of her walks that we met a woman who had a Labrador with her and was throwing a tennis ball for her dog. While doing that, she was also bragging about how fast her dog was. I took her challenge, removed

Roxie's leash, and had her throw the ball. Both dogs went after the ball and, of course, as I expected, Roxie beat the other dog to the ball.

I enjoyed the look on that woman's face. Her dog was twice the size of Roxie, yet she outpaced him and was not fazed by the size of her opponent. She was allowed to run, and she ran like the wind. She was always the one trying her best. She would run fast and try to run even faster than she ran previously. The same thing Roxie did with another one of her hobbies, which was jumping. Even though she was not a big dog, she could jump higher than most other dogs.

Nothing stopped her from being the best, in everything she did. I remember one incident when Roxie displayed a rare mood of her — impatience. I left her in the car to say hello to a friend, while she was selling some stuff outside of her apartment. Roxie, that crazy mutt, decided to rip up her jacket. I had to buy her a new one, and started training her not to tear stuff up, if she was feeling a bit off.

I mean everyone feels a bit every now and then, but that

is no reason to go tearing up stuff. Another time while Roxie was in a kennel, which as I have already mentioned she did not like, a next-door dog had a harness hanging, almost next to Roxie's stall, and like you would expect a hyper-energetic dog to do, she got a hold of that harness and shredded it to bits. Thankfully, after that incident, that dog's owner quickly learned to put her dog's harness, out of Roxie's reach.

Among the things that she loved to tear up and chew, was a fleece pad that I had put in her kennel, she tore that up too. That crazy mutt, whatever I put with her, would shred it, except for her play-toy that she could not destroy. I had a guest room in my condo where I had placed a twin bed for guests. It soon became one of Roxie's favorite places to hang out in the apartment, aside from my couch.

The reason for that was not the twin bed but the thing she did after jumping onto it, which was looking out of the window and barking at anyone who passed by. Even though her barks were more like playful yelps, she was disturbing the neighbors, and I quickly learned to keep the door of that room closed. Roxie, being a clever dog she was, learned fast that barking at people was a big no-no.

She was not one to overlook her mistakes. In fact, if she got to know that she had done something bad, she would punish herself and go sit in the bathtub, because she did not like to take baths and the tub was a place she did not like. I liked that about her. Roxie was free-spirited and did everything in that spirit. Of course, she was bound to slip up sometimes.

However, she never meant any harm by her actions. They just happened in the wrong instance. I always understood this about her, and dealt with patience everything that came up.

Chapter 10
The Last Days

I loved taking pictures of Roxie. She was very photogenic and had the uncanny ability to know, in which pose she would look her best. Whenever she saw me pointing a camera in her direction, she would strike a pose and not move, until she heard me call her. This was another thing I loved about her. She was amazing at having her pictures taken. There was this one time when I took her to the Art and Garden Center that is located in Ross, California, and it was right after someone's wedding. There were rose petals scattered on the stage, and the decorations were being taken down. The stage looked so pretty with the rose petals that I could not stop myself. I took a glass of wine, had Roxie sit on the stage beside the rose petals, and set the glass of wine down beside her.

The moment I took a picture of her, I think the wind shifted and sent the aroma of wine to Roxie, who turned her head toward me, and her nose turned up at the smell. It was the darnedest look. It was as if she was saying to me, *"Yuck mommy, do you drink that stuff?"* When Roxie turned 15 on June 10 in 2017, my co-workers gave her a party. She got a lot of stuff including toys. She was one happy girl that day, with all the treats and the attention she got.

As Roxie got older, her arthritis got worse. Even though it was mainly in her neck and back, she was hurting like hell. So I had Carey, who is a friend as well as a chiropractor, come over and work on her. Roxie felt so much better after Carey's visits. After Roxie turned 15, I upped her medication with the veterinarian's help and recommendation. As I went in to get a new and heavier dose of medication for her, the vet wanted to do some X-rays of her. But I felt that I did not want her to go for the X-rays. I felt she was too old and something bad might happen. As a result of this decision, the vet added another medication that would relieve her arthritis, as well as the muscles in her shoulder.

After January, I started leaving Roxie at home more and more, due to her age. The vet said that she was too old for any more vaccinations, including the flu shot. During my lunchtime, I started to go check up on her and administer her pain meds if she needed them. I would give her a second meal so that the medicine did not upset her stomach, after which I would return to work. When I got home from work in the evenings, I would give her another pain med around 4 p.m. After taking the medication, she would feel better, and usually eat her dinner of ground sirloin, which she loved with enthusiasm.

Sometimes, I would hand-feed her if she was hurting, even after the medication in her system. The lunch I would usually give her consisted of canned blue beef or crumbled Red Barn. It was easy for her to eat, since she had lost most of her teeth at that point in her life. As Roxie reached peak adulthood, becoming even older with each passing month, her neck began to hurt. It used to grow so sore that the poor dog could not handle wearing a collar on her neck. So, I stopped using the collar and leash altogether, as even the harness was too much for her to bear. I put a red coat on her and attached the leash to it, so that I could still take her out. The coat also did the job of keeping her warm. She was so weak at that time that she even had to wear the coat to bed. However, she did not leave her love for car rides behind, even in old age.

When she felt ok, I would often take her out in the car for a small ride. Even that was sometimes too much for her. To get her on the car, I had to use a footstool, so she did not have to jump into the car and land on her sore shoulder. In her adulthood, one of the favorite foods that Roxie loved was crackers. I used to get the one that had ham and cheese for my lunch as well, so both of us could share it.

If she did not eat well in the morning, I would give her some of my crackers at lunchtime. That was when she was at work with me. She would stand there and beg for those crackers. I think it was the salt and butter flavor of the crackers that she loved so much. I used to take Roxie for a long walk from the Ross Commons to Phoenix Lake and back to Ross where the car was. After her long walks and hikes, she would sleep for a few hours before getting up to have dinner. Then, I would take her out for her last walk of the day. As I have already said, she liked to sleep on my bed and would sometimes take up the whole bed. And then in the middle of the night, I would have to get her to go down to the foot of the bed so I could have some room.

It had become my routine to be ready in the morning, before I even got a chance to get up. Roxie would wait for me patiently until I was dressed and put a leash on her, after which she would proceed to rush to the door. Her expressions would be like, *"Hurry up, mom, I have gotten ready to go, don't want to be late for our work."*

Hence, I would take her down the stairs and to the gravel area. After which, we got into the car and would be off for work. The morning routine was followed by the afternoon routine. When we got home, she would once again want to go out for her walk, so I would take her around the block, which was one of her favorite walks and mine too. If no car was around, I would let her off the leash and have her follow me.

I did have to stop and look back for her, as she would sometimes stop to sniff at stuff along the way. Even though I tried to break her off that habit, it never worked. This was something she did all her life, the crazy mutt. Now, after Roxie is gone, every time I read her birthday cards and the sympathy cards I received from my workplace and my friends, I cry whenever I go through them, as I miss my crazy old mutt dearly.

I also look at her pictures, as she was very special, and I loved her so much. I wish dogs would live as long as we do. It is one of the hardest decisions to make when you have to put your best buddy to sleep, due to the pet's growing ill-health and frailty. It was February 8, when I went home to check up on her during my lunch hour as usual. It was time for her medication as well as lunch.

In the morning, when I had left for work, she was feeling okay and had eaten her breakfast, along with the medication. However, during lunchtime, when I went home to give her food and medicine, she was hurting really bad. This was alarming, considering Carey had worked his magic the night before.

I cannot forget that day for as long as I live. Roxie looked at me with so much pain in her little eyes, when I went to check up on her on that day during lunchtime.

It was as though she was telling me, *"Mommy, it's time for me to go away."*

Roxie gave me the strength to do what I had to do next. In the next few hours, I filled a syringe with some pain medication, dissolved in hot water, and managed to inject into my precious one in such a way that she would not be sore and hurting. I did all of this with a heavy heart.

I returned to work and called my vet, telling him that I would be bringing Roxie to the clinic on Thursday morning. I explained everything that was going on - the meds not working well anymore, and that she was too sore all over her little body. I also informed my supervisor about my decision to put Roxie to sleep.

She was really supportive and encouraged that I should take someone along for moral support, as this was not going to be easy. I asked Christina if she would like to drive me to the vet and she said yes. I also called my friends Laura and Carey to let them know and to see if they would like to say goodbye to her. For fifteen and a half years, both Laura and Carey had taken care of Roxie for me, when I had to go somewhere or work a night shift. They loved her as much as I did. Whenever Roxie went to Laura's place to stay, she would bring Roxie's favorite toy and blanket. Laura and Carey came over at about 10 p.m. to say goodbye to their friend, Roxie. Carey, Laura, and I were hoping that Roxie would get better with Carey's help, as she had been hurting the entire day. Yes, the therapy helped a lot, but it was only for a few hours.

Carey and Laura had brought Roxie her favorite food and hand-fed her while she stood up. That night, she had two dinners as well as snacks. I gave her the snacks after I gave her the medication, with the cheese from the cannelloni. It took several minutes before she ate it, as she hated her medication, but with the cheese, she finally ate and felt better after a few minutes.

I was able to give the rest of her medications to her, so she would not be hurting when Carey and Laura came over. They both stayed for a few hours, and Roxie finally fell asleep. Laura took some pictures of her with her iPhone, while Roxie lay on her bed. It was shortly after Roxie fell asleep that Laura and Carey left. Thursday morning, Roxie got up at about 6 a.m. and woke me up, trying to get comfortable on her bed. She was hurting badly. I gave her some pain medicine in her favorite ham and cream cheese, and thankfully, she ate it without a fuss. At 9 a.m., I gave her another half of her medicine so she would be comfortable. At about 10 a.m. or so, Christina came to take us to the vet, and I got Roxie's favorite toy, her rhinestone collar, her leash, and the heart necklace. I took the stool out to the car and put it by the back seat door.

I put the leash on Roxie and made her get on the car. Christina drove Roxie and me to the vet. I got the stool from the trunk, and Roxie got off the car for the last time. We took her to a room where I would be with her for the last time. Christina and I gave her treats and hugged her until the vet came in. He told me what he was going to do to put her to sleep. Even though I wanted to be with my girl till the end, I told the vet that I could not stay and watch.

I gave the vet her favorite toy collar and the necklace to go with her, when she was cremated. Christina and I left in tears. On the ride back, Christina took me to have a snack. When we got back to my condominium, I gave one of Roxie's bowls to Christina for helping me out. A couple of hours later, I had lunch with Kathy at the Woodland Café.

The next day, when I got back to work, there were cards and flowers from my co-workers at my desk. Dominica, who I worked with, gave me an orchid. I got sympathy cards from other people as well. To make me feel better, I began walking staff dogs. After a month of not having a dog in my place, I started taking care of other people's dogs for them.

I still remember the time when I got back to my condo after taking Roxie to the vet, I heard a squeaky little voice in my mind whispering, *"Thank you, mom, for letting me go. Now I can run like a youngster again."*

Sometimes, I even feel that I see her shadow going from my bedroom. Even though it might be wishful thinking, I still believe that Roxie is in a better place and from time to time she thinks of me, and that is when I catch glimpses of her out of the corner of my eyes.

After a few months, I went to Santa Rosa to be with my sister, who took me out to lunch. While we were talking, she was the one who came up with the idea, for me to write a book about Roxie. When I met Roxie, I had no idea that she was going to play such a big part of my life. After I had lost my friend and companion, I would place flowers by her picture after every two weeks… in remembrance of that crazy mutt. It has been several months now, and I still read 15 years' worth of her birthday cards, as well as the sympathy cards I got after she was gone. I also look at the pictures I took of her over the years. Every time I see these things, I still cry. I will always remember her craziness, and her love for me. When people see how much I still miss Roxie, they always ask me if I will get another dog.

I tell them *"Yes, but the new dog can never replace Roxie."*

Roxie was special and in my heart, I believe that someday I will see her again. Thank you Roxie for sharing your life with me. You will be missed, and you will always be in my heart. Here is a poem that I want to share in loving memory of my friend and longtime companion.

The Last Battle

If it should be that I grow frail and weak
And pain should keep me from my sleep,
Then will you do what must be done,
For this -- the last battle -- can't be won.
You will be sad I understand,
But don't let grief then stay your hand.
For on this day, more than the rest
Your love and friendship must stand the test.
We have had so many happy years,
You wouldn't want me to suffer so.
When the time comes, please, let me go.
Take me to where to my needs they'll tend,
Only, stay with me till the end
And hold me firm and speak to me
Until my eyes no longer see.
I know in time you will agree
It is a kindness you do to me.
Although my tail its last has waved,
From pain and suffering I have been saved.
Don't grieve that it must be you
Who has to decide this thing to do.

We've been so close -- we two -- these years,
  Don't let your heart hold any tears.

-*Julia Napier*